C000184099

Shirley

Madeira

Walks

Shirley Whitehead's Madeira Walks
First Edition - November 2006 **Copyright** © 2006

Published by
Discovery Walking Guides Ltd
10 Tennyson Close, Northampton NN5 7HJ,
England

Maps
Map sections are adapted from **Madeira Tour &
Trail Map 4th edition** (ISBN 1-904946-26-7)
published by Discovery Walking Guides Ltd, and
are resized to 1:25,000 scale map sections.

Front Cover Photographs

Walk 5

Walk 11

Walk 8

Walk 13

ISBN 1-904946-31-3 (9781904946311)
Text and photographs © Shirley Whitehead
Maps © David & Ros Brawn

Shirley Whitehead's Madeira Walks

CONTENTS

THE WALKS

APPENDICES

Meet the Author

Shirley Whitehead settled in Madeira in 2002. Born in Lancashire England, she lived for many years in West Yorkshire where she developed a keen interest in the natural and built environment and walked extensively in the Yorkshire Dales as well as the Peak and Lake Districts.

During that time she was involved with various wildlife and environmental charities, was a member of the British Wild Flower Society and the National Trust and Secretary of the Halifax Civic Trust.

Along with her husband Michael, she has travelled widely and driven overland through Lapland, Tanzania, Zimbabwe and Zambia as well as undertaking walking and camping safaris in the Zambezi Valley, the Udzungwa Mountains and Chitwan National Park, Nepal.

Since moving to Madeira she has pursued these interests vigorously discovering the island's diverse landscape and vegetation; walking levada paths, forest trails, moorland and mountain tracks and coastal routes, accompanied by her Border Collie Lucy. She is a regular contributor to the Madeira Times, writing articles on walking and heritage and lives in the south west of the island.

Visit www.discovermadeira.homestead.com

Preface

This book came about as a result of my passion for walking and the natural environment, and where better to pursue these interests than in Madeira. Whether you walk for pleasure, health, a challenge or a combination of these, this island offers it all. I have personally walked all the routes in this book plus many more on the island and I believe that my selection covers some of the most beautiful walks I have encountered and offers a range of routes from gentle rambles to those covering more challenging terrain.

At this juncture I would like to add that I do not consider myself an expert walker, but would rather describe myself as a serious nature lover. I walk for pleasure and of course to explore the island, and I like to take in my surrounding rather than undertake a strenuous route march. Also when walking I like to feel confident and safe; I don't take unnecessary risks nor push myself beyond my capabilities; I work on the theory that walking should be about enjoying the best aspects of the landscape whilst minimizing on effort, so whenever possible I avoid steep ascents and difficult terrain. Therefore, in documenting these walks I have tried to give a first hand account of the experience, the location and the terrain as well as good directions for getting to starting points, which will no doubt be important to anyone new to the island. Where possible I have also included information on the flora and fauna in each area, particularly in relation to endemic species as well as providing information on local landmarks, historic buildings and rural communities within each vicinity.

As a result, this selection of walks provides something for everyone, regardless of individual ability and fitness, so that everyone can enjoy walking in Madeira as an independent experience, undertaking the routes in their own time and at their own pace without the demands that group walking or guide led walks can make.

Finally, no walking guide can be fully comprehensive, and particularly so in Madeira where there are more walks than can ever be contained in one book. As a result, this book has been designed as a companion to **Walk! Madeira** (also published by Discovery Walking Guides Ltd); the two focusing largely on different geographical areas across the island. The walks in this publication are concentrated mainly in the West and Central West regions with some coverage of other parts of the island. **"Walk! Madeira"** providing coverage of the East, North and Central areas as well as the Funchal district.

Enjoy walking in Madeira and enjoy your holiday…

Shirley & Lucy near Encumeada

Acknowledgement
I would like to thank David and Ros Brawn of Discovery Walking Guides Ltd for accepting these walks for publication providing me with a medium for sharing my passion for walking and natural history

INTRODUCTION

Madeira Island

Looking down on Funchal harbour

Madeira Island, part of Portugal, is situated in the Eastern Atlantic approximately 600 kms west of Morocco and 1000 kms south of Lisbon, and together with the Azores, the Canaries and Cape Verde Islands, forms a bio-geographic region referred to as Macaronesia.

The Madeira archipelago consists of Madeira Island, Porto Santo, 40 kms north east, The Desertas Islands, 13 kms south, and The Selvagens, which although 300 kms south east, are still administered by the Autonomous Region of Madeira. Madeira proper covers an area of 737 kms^2 being 57 kms east-west and 23 kms north-south and has a resident population of c 248,500. The capital of Madeira is Funchal; a beautiful city lying on the south coast, which rises to 600 mtrs from the coastline up the mountain ridges, creating a stunning first impression when arriving on the island. Porto Santo is approximately 42 kms^2 being 12 kms east-west and 5 kms north-south with a population of around 5000, and is renowned for its magnificent sandy beach stretching 7 kms along the southern coast. The Desertas Islands (Reserva Natural das Ilhas Desertas) and the Selvagens (Reserva Natural das Ilhas Selvagens) are uninhabited nature reserves protected by the Parque Natural da Madeira.

Landscape & Climate

Madeira enjoys a temperate climate throughout the year with average daytime temperatures around the coast of 18–24 degrees. However, in common with many mountainous islands it experiences numerous micro-climates. The south coast is the sunniest and driest with cooler, damper weather in the north. The mountain regions are subject to rapid changes often becoming wild, wet and cloudy with the occurrence of snow on the high

Jardim do Mar
from Prazeres

peaks in winter.

The island is volcanic, although long extinct, and one of its greatest tourist attractions is its spectacular landscape; rugged and mountainous with luxurious vegetation. The central mountain range extends across most of its length with the highest mountain Pico Ruivo rising to 1860 m (6100 ft). 90% of the island stands at more than 500 m above sea level with much of the coastline characterized by high cliffs and fajãs (narrow flat low lying areas between the sea and cliffs). Cabo Girão on the south coast stands at 580 m and is the second highest cape in the world.

Paúl da Serra

A large percentage of the island is wild and uninhabited and is protected by The Parque Natural da Madeira; this includes the Mountain Range, the Laurel Forests (*Laurisilva*), the Ancient Heath Forests, the upland plateau of Paúl da Serra, the São Lourenço Peninsula in the east, as

São Lourenço Peninsula

well as some other coastal areas. The Pine and Eucalyptus Forests, at a lower altitude, are the responsibility of the Forestry Service operating from the Postos Florestais which are dotted around the island, often in remote areas. The inhabited areas are concentrated around the coast line with the agricultural terraces sweeping down the mountain slopes to the coast which, in the rural areas, is dotted with small agricultural and fishing villages. The island is fertile and sub-tropical with an amazing and diverse flora; no wonder it is often referred to as "the floating garden of the Atlantic". The farming areas have been cultivated over the centuries and produce bananas, grapes and a vast array of tropical fruits and vegetables. The indigenous and naturalized flowers and trees grow side by side and will fascinate all those who are drawn to nature.

Bananas

Another important feature of Madeira's landscape, and a major tourist attraction drawing in walkers from around the world, is the unique levada network which spans most of the island enabling penetration into the interior, which would otherwise be impossible.

The Laurisilva

The natural forest of Madeira is the largest area of Laurisilva in the world. It covers 150 sq. kms (58 sq miles) representing just over 20% of the island's surface. Many of the plants evolved millions of years ago and the Laurisilva survives now only in Central Macaronesia (Azores, Madeira and Western Canaries). These are sub-tropical humid forests influenced by the mist and growing in the cloud zone at 300 – 1300 mtrs in the north and 700 – 1200 mtrs in the south and, due to their importance, were classified a World Nature Heritage Site in 1999 by UNESCO

The Levada Network

The levada network is unique to Madeira and consists of a series of irrigation channels creating an ingenious watering system across the island. The channels cover a distance of 2100 kms (1300 miles) including 30 kms of tunnels, and were designed to carry water from the wetter and humid areas in the north to provide irrigation in the arid agricultural areas in the south. These water channels, of Arabian influence, were constructed over a period of five centuries, initially by slave labour from Africa, Arabia and the Canaries. At first privately owned, they were taken into public control and enhanced in the early 1900's. The paths alongside the

Levada da Bica da Cana

channels are shaped to the demands of the local topography and are often carved through the rock face. Some are wide and comfortable for walking, while others follow precarious ledges along the channels. The levadas run along the mountain sides, through ravines and forests and extend down to the agricultural terraces and as well as supporting rich natural vegetation, they are often well planted with agapanthus, hydrangea and other species, creating wonderful banks of colour along their route. The Levadeiros (Levada Workers) are charged with keeping the levadas and paths in good condition and the Levada Keepers cottages, usually with well planted gardens, can be found along many of the routes.

Levada Nova Prazeres

THE ISLAND'S FLORA & FAUNA

Trees and Flowers

Due to island's climate and fertility Madeira is a botanical paradise renowned for its luxurious vegetation. The first species to be noticed when you arrive on the island will be the tropical palms and cycads and the attractive flowering plants which have been introduced and cultivated along the roadside verges providing

Bird of Paradise

year round colour. These include Agapanthus, and Hydrangea, which flower during the summer months, the Bird of Paradise (Strelitzia)

Sword Aloe

from South Africa; which flowers most of the year round and the Red Sword Aloa which flanks the roadsides in winter. In the parks, gardens and avenues of Funchal you will find the Flamingo Flower (Anthurium), Protea and many varieties of Orchids together with many magnificent flowering trees, including the African Tulip Tree, the Blue Jacaranda, Flame Trees and Kapoc Trees which will not fail to impress. There are also a number of wonderful Agavaceae on the island, including the amazing Swan's Neck (Agava attenuata) growing on the verges around the airport and the magnificent Spanish Dagger (Yucca gloriosa) which can be found in the parks and gardens.

Spanish Dagger

In the natural environment, there are said to be 1340 species of indigenous and naturalized vascular plants (excluding pure garden varieties in parks and gardens). Almost 800 are indigenous and around 15% of these are endemic species, occurring nowhere else in the world.[*1] The remainder are foreign species introduced as ornamental plants or for food or wood production, and which have now naturalized. Of the endemic plants, there are too many wonderful species to mention, but perhaps Pride of Madeira is one the most spectacular with one species (Echium nervosum) growing along the coast line

Shrubby Sow Thistle

Pride of Madeira

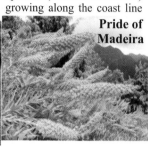

and a second (Echium candicans) confined to the mountain areas. Also of particular interest are the three species of Shrubby Sow Thistle (Sonchus sp.), these are better described as giant Dandelions; they are tree and shrub size and grow in ravines in the forest and at altitudes above 600 mtrs; they are quite unique. Other endemics not to be missed are the wild geraniums, the Madeira Crane's-Bill and the Anemone-Leaved Crane's-Bill, the former again growing to the size of a large bush. One of the rare species of the Laurisilva is the Yellow Foxglove (Isoplexis sceptrum) related to the European purple foxglove, which is a joy to discover. Another species worthy of mention is the magnificent Macaronesian endemic, the Dragon Tree (Dracaena draco), another of the Agavaceae family, which originally thrived on Porto Santo and the São Lourenço Peninsula but which is now almost extinct; the only ones surviving naturally found near to Ribeira Brava. Nevertheless many can be seen in

Yellow Foxglove

the parks and gardens around the island but the most impressive display is at Núcleo de Dragoeiros das Neves Nature Centre near São Gonçalo, which is definitely worth a visit. (See section on Natural History Museums, Parks and Gardens for details).

Dragon Trees

Of the indigenous vegetation of the Laurisilva, there are around 20 different tree species, four of which belong to the Laurel family (Lauraceae). All these species are evergreen except for the deciduous Canary Willow and most are extremely difficult to identify due to the similarity of their flat, leathery leaves. The endemic tree species of the Laurisilva include: - the Lily of the Valley Tree (Clethra arborea), Madeira Holly (Ilex perado), Madeira Bilberry (Vaccinium padifolium) and the Carrot Tree (Monizia edulis)

Forestation on the lower mountain slopes, particularly in the south, has been taken over with pine, acacia and eucalyptus, which although introduced, have now naturalized in these areas. This is as a result of human intervention over the centuries, making way for agriculture, and the eucalyptus in particular has become so invasive it is now beginning to threaten the territory of the indigenous forests.

[*1] **P. Sziemer - Madeira's Natural History in a Nutshell**

Birds

In terms of bird population, Madeira has a relatively low count, with around 42 breeding species plus migrant visitors. The only true endemics are the Long-toed Pigeon which inhabits the Laurisilva and the Madeira Storm Petrel which breeds on the cliff tops. There are however a number of endemic varieties such as the Madeira Firecrest, Madeira Chaffinch and Grey Wagtail as well as Macaronesian endemic varieties including the Canary, Berthelot's Pipit, Plain Swifts and Blackcaps.

SPEA-Madeira - The Portuguese Society for the Protection of Birds, a partner of Birdlife International, has produced two leaflets covering bird life in the Laurisilva and Ponta do Pargo IBA's

(Important Bird Areas defined by Birdlife International). These can be obtained from Tourist Offices and the Madeira Story Centre in the Old Town. For details of publications see Appendix B.

Animals

There are no mammals other than bats occurring naturally on the island, however those introduced include rabbits and goats and a number of small rodents such as rats and mice, and of course domestic animals, sheep and cattle. Grazing land being rather

A familiar sight on the ER110

scarce on Madeira, you will often find cattle roaming on the roads and moorland on the southern slopes of Paúl da Serra. There are a number of reptiles (although thankfully no snakes) with the only endemic species being the Madeiran Wall Lizard (Teira dugesii) Insects include grasshoppers, crickets and migratory Locusts plus many butterflies, of which, the Madeira Brimstone and Madeira Speckled Wood are endemic. Aquatic mammals include a

Madeira Wall Lizard

number of species of Whales and Dolphins which can sometimes be observed from the coastal areas. Also worth a special mention is the endangered Mediterranean Monk Seal one of the worlds most threatened mammals, but which now thrive around on the Desertas Islands and are occasionally seen on the Madeiran coast. Of the Aquatic Reptilia, Turtles are also a thriving species and are quite commonly seen in the coastal waters.

WALKING

Before you start

Preparation
Be prepared – read through the walk descriptions before starting out and note the information for each route and if you are new to Madeira, I suggest you start with a shorter, gentler route. Grades and timings are given at the start of each walk and any difficult sections are identified within the text. The terrain on the routes varies widely, some levada walks, although long, are invariably flat and easy, whilst others require more concentration if the channel shoulder is narrow, or precipitous drops are unprotected. Anyone suffering from vertigo or from poor balance should heed the warnings given and if in doubt, walkers should turn back if they are uncomfortable with the more challenging sections of levada paths.

Weather
On most days the weather in Madeira is clear and calm, but the island owes its lush landscape to the damp, mild climate and the island's topography can result in one area being bathed in sunshine whilst another is experiencing low cloud or heavy showers. The levadas are not really a problem during the summer period as the routes are clear and defined. However, during the winter months levada walks can become difficult due to landslips and heavy rain, making the surfaces unsafe or sometimes impassable; always turn back if conditions are bad. In the mountain areas, you should be aware that the weather is constantly subject to rapid change and mists can quickly invade the valleys and reduce viability. As a general quide, it is better to start out early if planning a high altitude walk, as the cloud tends to build up in the afternoons, and to avoid disappointment it is always a good idea to decide on a back-up walk at a lower altitude, should visibility be bad when you arrive at your chosen destination.

Safety

There is no organized mountain rescue service on Madeira; any incidents having to be dealt with by the emergency services; a

combination of Ambulance, Fire and Police. 23 trails across the island have been, or are in the process of being, signed at the starting points, giving details of the terrain, altitude, expected weather conditions, walking times etc. This project, known as Tourmac, covering walking routes in the three Macaronesia regions of Madeira, the Azores and the Canaries, has been funded in Madeira by the Regional Government and the European INTERREG 111 Programme.

Importantly these signs clearly state that no responsibility whatsoever is accepted for personal injury or loss or damage of property by those walking these routes. We can therefore assume that this applies to all footpaths on the island. Therefore, it goes without saying that everyone is individually responsible for their own safety and as such should take adequate precautions and follow a common sense code. The following information is offered.

- Keep to the routes given
- Always let someone know where you are heading and your expected time of return
- Wear suitable footwear and clothing
- Turn back if bad weather sets in
- Don't take risks
- Take lots of water with you, and food on longer walks
- Always carry sun cream

- If possible, take a mobile phone and emergency contact numbers

Clothing and Equipment

Many of the walks included in this series are along the levada footpaths and require little in terms of equipment; I find that excess weight can be a real burden and spoils the enjoyment. However, I offer a few guidelines for those routes at higher altitudes and those with more challenging terrain.

- Wear comfortable clothing and carry a Micro fleece and light raincoat if walking in the mountains.
- Always wear good footwear, either walking boots or rugged walking sandals.
- Walking poles are advisable for rough terrain and steep ascents and descents, but are not necessary on the levada paths.
- A torch is a must for most of the levada tunnels. Don't forget the spare batteries.
- Take along sun cream, water, and food for longer journeys. Most of the walks have nowhere en-route to buy refreshments.
- For navigation, take a good guide book, map and possibly a whistle.
- A small basic medical kit may be useful, but I have to admit that I do not take one along
- If possible take a mobile phone with emergency numbers

Getting Around

Hire cars and taxis are the most convenient way of getting around and since the completion of the Rapido, (the new highway), with its amazing network of tunnels and bridges, accessibility to all areas of the island is relatively quick and easy.

Car Hire

Hire cars, at competitive rates, are available at the airport and from hotels and agencies in Funchal as well as from other towns around the island.

Taxis

For those not wanting to drive, a taxi is the best alternative solution. Drivers will take you to the start of each walk and, if required, will collect you at the end of the walk. Taxis can be hired for half or full days and drivers carry standard price lists for journeys outside of Funchal. Telephone numbers for rural taxis to link with this series of walks, can be found at Appendix A.

Local Buses

The island bus companies also provide an excellent service and there are special tickets that make this good value. Due to frequent changes in services, I have not included bus schedules in this book. However timetables are available from Newsagents Kiosks and from the Tourist Offices around the island. There is also a good link on the Madeira-Island website covering rural bus routes and timetables; visit www.madeira-island.com/bus.services. Finally, I also recommend the Madeira Bus and Touring Map produced by Discovery Walking Guides Ltd., which provides an invaluable resource for both bus users and car drivers.

MAP INFORMATION

Map Sections for Walking Routes

The map sections used to illustrate the detailed walk descriptions in *Shirley Whitehead's Madeira Walks* are developed from the latest 4th edition of the Madeira Tour & Trail Super-Durable Map.

For each of Shirley's walks we have redrawn our Tour & Trail digital database to show Shirley's route as a Red dashed line with alternatives and other published walking routes shown as a Green dashed line. The Red and Green dashed lines are drawn alongside the feature they refer to; eg path, track, road etc.

Once the new Shirley Whitehead version of the digital database is completed, the map design is resized to the popular 1:25,000 scale familiar to UK walkers. On all the map sections illustrating the detailed walk descriptions 1 Kilometre is 4 Centimetres.

Having produced the 1:25,000 map sections we then add the 'Start' and 'Finish' logos to complete each individual map section that is used in this book.

Madeira Tour & Trail Super-Durable Map 4th edition was comprehensively updated in 2006 based on a new ground survey by David & Ros Brawn.

WALKS IN THE WEST REGION
1 Levada Nova - Fajã da Ovelha to Ponta do Pargo
2 Levada Nova - Ponta do Pargo to Cabo
3 Levada Nova - Prazeres to Estrela da Calheta
4 Prazeres to Paúl do Mar & Jardim do Mar
5 Levada Nova - Loreto, Arco da Calheta to Canhas, Ponta do Sol
6 Lombada da Ponta do Sol - Levada Nova & Levada Moinha

WALKS IN THE CENTRAL (WEST) REGION
7 The Tunnel and Trail to 25 Fontes
8 To Risco Waterfall
9 Ribeira Grande Valley - Rabaçal
10 Off the beaten track in Paúl da Serra
11 The Southern Slopes of Paúl da Serra - Cristo Rei along Levada da Bica da Cana
12 The Southern Slopes of Paúl da Serra - Cristo Rei to Fátima Chapel - Rabaçal
13 Bica da Cana to Pináculo
14 Encumeada - The Lily of the Valley Trail to Folhadal
15 Encumeada - Levada do Norte & Levada das Rabaças

WALKS IN THE EAST & NORTH EAST REGION

17 Ponta de São Lourenço Peninsula - Baia d'Abra to Casa do Sardinha
18 Ribeira de São Roque Valley - Faial - Levada do Castelejo
19 Ribeira de São Roque Valley - Faial - Levada do Baixol
20 Ribeiro Frio to Portela

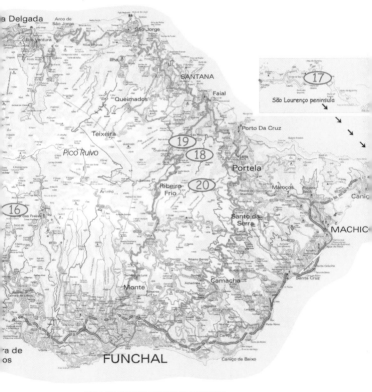

WALKS IN THE CENTRAL REGION

16 Boca da Corrida to Pico Grande

Walk 1   Levada Nova – Fajã da Ovelha to Ponta do Pargo

Walking time:
2 hrs 45 mins from the ER223 Fajã da Ovelha to Ponta do Pargo Village Centre. **Note:** This stretch of the Levada Nova crosses over the ER101 in three further locations along the road, providing alternative options for shortening this route.

Grade
Easy walking along a level levada path with a descent of 110 m down a tarred road into the village centre of Ponta do Pargo.

Directions and Starting Point:
Follow the new R101 from Ribeira Brava to its termination in Prazeres turning left onto the ER101 signed Porto Moniz and

Ponta do Pargo. Continue for 4.8 km until you reach a left turn signed Fajã da Ovelha/Paúl do Mar (ER223). The levada crosses the Fajã road approx 100 mtrs from the turn off and can be seen on the right. Parking is available at this point

Note: The 12 km section of the ER101 from Prazeres to Ponta do Pargo will be renumbered ER222 following completion of the final phase of the new highway from late 2006 onwards.

Since the opening of the new highway, the west of the island is now easily accessible and fast becoming a favourite with many walkers. Prazeres is only 30 mins from Funchal and so for this walk I have chosen a section of Levada Nova. I say section because Levada Nova extends some 50 kms along the south west coast of Madeira from its source above Ponta do Sol to its termination in Cabo (a parish of Ponta do Pargo at the far western point of the island). The channel flows at a height of around 600 mtrs and throughout its length the path contours the southern slopes of the western mountain range, through deep valley heads and narrow ravines as well as forested and agricultural areas. Over the last three years I have walked the whole of Levada Nova by breaking it down into manageable sections and so I have come to

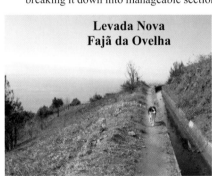

Levada Nova
Fajã da Ovelha

know the most beautiful, dramatic and isolated areas which are a joy to walk. The terrain along the whole of my chosen route makes for comfortable and easy walking with no dangerous or precipitous drops along the way and is therefore suitable for most abilities.

From the starting point pick up the levada on the right of the road and follow down stream where the route takes us through the pine forest and along the hillside high above Fajã da Ovelha. After 15 mins the path passes in front of a large house and

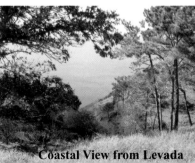

Coastal View from Levada

crosses over the access road where the channel has been culverted for a short stretch. The levada is picked up again down a short flight of steps and now continues around the open hillside. Along most of the trail the levada is flanked by bracken, bramble and gorse and you are immediately aware of the Madeira Wall Lizards scurrying into the undergrowth. The channel crosses a number of small valley heads dipping in and out of the Pine and Eucalyptus forests and shortly after crosses another narrow road leading down from São João following which, the lighthouse at Ponta do Pargo and the village of Amparo come into view. After a total of 50 mins walking you now find yourself above the new road leading into Fajãda Ovelha and at this point the levada crosses over the ER101 and is picked up on the opposite side of the road. The path now meanders around another valley head before doubling back and again crossing the ER101 just below the village of Lombada dos Marinheiros where you now find yourself skirting the southern agricultural terraces of this rural village. A little further along, the channel again crosses the ER101 at a picnic and barbeque site approximately 1.5 kms before the village of Amparo. This second section takes around 45 mins in total. Following the levada from the picnic site you now pass through small hamlets with apple orchards and orange groves before traversing around a number of valley heads where lush vegetation and mixed woodland take over. Here you will find Sweet Chestnut, Oak, Maple, Walnut, Acacia and Laurels. A little further along the landscape then opens up to lower shrub land allowing views of the coastline along most of the remainder of the route.

During the winter months the flowers along this route are sparse, but in spring and summer the footpath is flanked with an exuberance of cultivated and wild flowers including Agapanthus and Hydrangea as well as Honeysuckle, Madeira Crane's-Bill, Sweet Violets, Calla Lilies and Morning Glory just to mention a few. Also not to be missed is the frequent appearance of damsel flies, Monarch butterflies (Danaus plexippus) and the Clouded Yellow (Colias crocea) flitting between the plants and in the cooler weather, the Migratory Locust (Locusta migratoria) can also be seen. The whole route is tranquil and peaceful and I have observed birds of prey and many other species which inhabit this coastal area.

This final section takes around 40 mins ending above the village of Ponta do Pargo at a large water tank and water treatment building on the left. (Don't confuse this with an earlier water tank, again on the left above Amparo). Leave the levada here passing between the tank and building emerging onto a tarred road which you follow right for approximately 1 km to arrive in the village centre at Ponta do Pargo; a descent of 110 metres. Taxis and buses are available in the village centre to take you back to your starting point.

O Farol Ponta do Pargo

If completing the whole walk, you may also wish to drop down to the Miradouro at Casa de Chá restaurant and to the lighthouse (Farol) a little further along. Both are situated on the headland approximately 1 km below the village on a further descent of 150 mtrs. (Allow an extra 20 mins). The landscape around the Farol is wild open grassland, the coastline is magnificent and in spring the wild flowers are a delight.

Alternative option

Should you prefer a shorter and more relaxed walk I recommend a ramble along the first section between the two roads leading to Fajãda Ovelha and then retracing your steps back to the starting point and combining the day out with a drive along the ER223 into Paul do Mar. This mountain road which descends steeply into Paúl is one of the most spectacular on Madeira and along its route negotiates three short tunnels. Take time to stop at the church of Fajã da Ovelha, a lovely building of Moorish influence with its walled cemetery and huge Date Palms. At Paúl do Mar, drive to the far end of the village and take a right fork to the new harbour (just before the Jardim do Mar road tunnel). Once there, feel the buzz of this lovely traditional fishing village; its position beneath the cliffs is stunning. There are a number of bars and restaurants in the area and a wander through the enchanting narrow streets with the traditional Portuguese architecture is a must. Also spectacular, is the new bronze statue erected on a rock looking out to sea; a tribute to fishermen past and present.

Walk 2   Levada Nova – Ponta do Pargo to Cabo

Walking time:
Circular route total time 3 hrs
Grade:
Easy walking, first along a wide concrete road, and latterly on sandy or asphalt lanes. The approach to Levada Nova from the hamlet of Pedregal requires an ascent of approximately 150m, but an alternative route is suggested for those not wanting to attempt this climb. The shoulder of the Levada Nova is good, with a wide level path and no precipitous drops. Other than the initial climb, this route is suitable for all abilities.
Directions and Starting Point:-
Follow directions for Walk 1 to Prazeres village. From here take the ER101 west signed Porto Moniz and Ponta do Pargo and continue for 14 kms until you reach the centre of Ponta do Pargo. As you approach the end of the village leave the regional road taking a left turn signed Pico das Favas and Farol. A few metres ahead you meet the village road which descends down to the Lighthouse (Farol). Park around this junction and follow a concrete road which descends off to the right running parallel to the ER 101.

This is a circular walk in the most westerly part of the island, starting in the parish of Ponta do Pargo and taking in the final section of the Levada Nova (approx 5 kms) to the hamlet of Cabo at the boundary of the of Calheta and Porto Moniz districts.

From the centre of Ponta do Pargo village at the junction of the regional ER101 and the village road which leads down to the lighthouse, take a concrete road which descends off to the right running almost parallel to the ER1O1. The road contours the first valley and after 20 minutes brings you into Pedregal, a pretty hamlet with traditional buildings and well tended gardens where magnificent displays of Wisteria and Jasmine greeted me on my visit there in spring. In the centre of the hamlet, just past a well on the right, take a right turn up a tarred road which eventually crosses the ER101. During spring and early summer look out for the endemic Madeira Crane's-Bill (Geranium maderense) which grows around this the area; this is not just a simple Geranium, it's almost a bush, with an abundance of cerise flower heads; one of the wonderful endemic giant species of Madeira. Crossing the main road, continue up the hill, at first on a cobbled lane which becomes an earthen track after the last little Madeiran house. Now continue up the hill through Pine and Eucalyptus forests until a fork in the road. Taking either direction, both tracks soon pass over the levada. The climb from Pedregal hamlet to the levada is approximately 150 mtrs and takes a good half hour, so beware if it is a hot day, it can be quite a pull. From here follow the levada downstream around a number of valley heads crossing streams and forest tracks along the way. As the forested area thins out, you can take in the wonderful views of the coastline, the lighthouse at Ponta do Pargo and Pico da Favas (a small volcanic mound with a high mast, set against the lovely oceanic views). To the north lie

the mountain slopes, albeit these are much lower in the west of the island. I walked this route on a beautiful day when the sea and sky were a brilliant blue and wild flowers, birds and butterflies were in

View from Levada Nova

abundance. This side of the island is so quiet, peaceful and unspoiled and the levada path is flanked with the natural vegetation of bramble, gorse and broom interspersed with Laurels and Mimosas as well as the deciduous Maples and Oaks displaying their bright green spring foliage.

After approximately 55 minutes the levada crosses over the regional ER101 road arriving 5 minutes later at a water tank on a tarred road leading down to the hamlet of Cabo. Turn left here and descend down the road until you reach the lovely solitary Capela of Nossa Senhora da Boa Morte above the headland. This is such a beautiful spot. The original building dates from the early 17th century but was rebuilt in more recent times.

Nossa Senhora da Boa Morte

Nevertheless many original features still remain with the architectural style typical Portuguese. The chapel is only open at certain times (you need to check opening times at the church in Ponta do Pargo), but if possible try to view the interior. It is really lovely with its Baroque alter and lovely furnishings. From the chapel, a narrow concrete

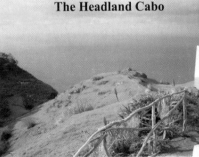

The Headland Cabo

path leads down across a low grassy area to a Miradouro on the edge of the cliffs allowing fine views along the coastline as well as providing a wonderful setting for an en-route picnic.

Back at the car park beside the church, now follow an earthen road which maintains height and contours around a small valley eventually going left through woodland with further views of the sea. This path leads on to the hamlet of Lombada Velha where it meets a tarred road leading down from the ER101 into the village. However, five minutes before you reach the village it is well worth doing a short detour on a right hand path which leads to a trig point on the cliff top. The vegetation here is mainly low shrub land where the forestation thins out and the path passes disused agricultural land where giant reeds and a variety of vegetation have taken over. The view from the trig point is stunning. The sea is brilliant turquoise and crystal clear and the cliffs are so majestic. The whole detour takes only 10 minutes, so it's well worth it. Back on the original path, continue on to Lombada Velha and once at the tarred road turn right through the village. After a steep descent at the end of the village, the road veers left and then onto the next hamlet where another detour to the right takes you down to a derelict building surrounded by trees. This can be easily recognised as the house is surrounded by a copse of trees including a number of large Date Palms, and the largest tree, a Eucalyptus,

The Old School and Copse

has a pretty shrine set into its trunk, it's definitely worth a peep. Apparently this building was a former school, confirmed to me by an elderly Portuguese man I had met back in the village. He had returned to his home in Madeira after spending almost 50 years in South Africa and had attended this school as a child. Back on the road continue right down another slope where the road crosses Ribeira da Vaca before continuing up hill to the hamlet of Serrada. Worthy of note at this point, are the traditional Portuguese houses, many now derelict and abandoned but displaying elegant and ornate carvings around the doors and windows. From Serrada, keep to the right and continue along the road until you again reach Pedregal passing the road we originally turned into, and then continue back to the starting point in Ponta do Pargo. The walk from Cabo back to Ponta do Pargo is around 4 kms and takes approximately one hour excluding the detours.

Alternative suggestion:-
For those not wishing to tackle the climb up to Levada Nova, I suggest walking on the lower road to Cabo in both directions. This runs at approximately 450 mtrs and other than a few ups and downs, provides for an easier and more leisurely walk leaving time to drop down to the Lighthouse and the Miradouro at Ponta do Pargo or perhaps end the day with a drink at Casa de Chá, a lovely little tea shop and restaurant on the cliff top. The landscape at this westerly point is quite unlike that which we most associate with Madeira. For me it is reminiscent of the Northumberland coastline or perhaps St. David's Head in Southern Wales. It is quite and wild, yet so gentle and green. I always enjoy my visits here; the coastline is so magnificent.

Walk 3   Levada Nova – Prazeres to Estrela da Calheta

Walking Time:
Option One - Prazeres to Atalhinho Water House - 2 hrs 30 mins return.
Option Two - Prazeres to Estrela da Calheta 4 hrs one way.

Grade:
An easy grade walk along the levada shoulder with no precipitous places. Option 2 necessitates a final descent of 300 mtrs down the ER211 leading into the centre of Estrela da Calheta where taxis and buses are available.

Directions and Starting Point:-
Follow directions for Walk 1 to Prazeres village and from here take the ER222 east signed Funchal. After 200 mtrs, at the village cross roads, take a left turn on the ER210 signed Paúl da Serra and Fonte do Bispo. The Levada Nova crosses the road approx 100 mtrs along, just above the Forestry House (Posta Florestal). Roadside parking is available at this point. The church and Quinta Pedagógica are situated in the village centre and the Farmers Market "Merçado dos Agricultores" can be found south of the village and is well signed from all directions.

The parish of Prazeres is possibly one of the least known on the island yet is undoubtedly one of the most picturesque. To the north the village borders the Parque Natural da Madeira and is set against a spectacular backdrop of forest and mountains, making walking in this area extremely popular. The village centre of

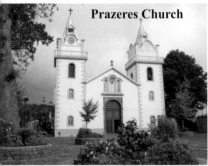
Prazeres Church

Prazeres also has lots to offer the visitor; the lovely twin-spired village church, built in the 18th century, albeit later transformed in 1922, is dedicated to Nossa Senhora de Neves (Our Lady of the Snow) and it is well worth a visit. Also not to be missed is the adjoining Quinta Pedagógica and Casa de Chá which offers a parish

zoo, a beautiful herb garden and a tea house. The menagerie includes Emu, Llama, Bambi and miniature ponies as well as many unusual species of swine and water foul and the Tea House provides a wide selection of herbal teas, preserves, cider and plants for sale to the public. This enterprise was an initiative of the church, funded by the European Community Fund to aid employment in this agricultural area, and it now provides a lovely facility for visitors. Also highly popular with residents and tourists alike, is the Sunday Farmers Market where you can buy a wide range of freshly grown vegetables, fruit and flowers, as well as freshly baked bread, cakes and handicrafts. So

Quinta Pedagógica Herb Garden

combining a visit to this lovely village with a ramble in the idyllic surroundings is highly recommended. However I digress, so let's make a start on the walk.

The Levada Nova flows a few hundred metres from the village centre just above the Forestry House on the ER210. It is one of the longest irrigation channels on the island, and this section winds alongside the mountain slopes through the national park maintaining its height at 600 mtrs. Starting on the opposite side of the road to the Forestry House, follow the levada upstream, first passing through a small inhabited area but soon entering the forest leaving the village behind. The first section is given over to pine and eucalyptus and the path is planted with Lily of the Nile (Agapanthus) and Hydrangea. Clearly the conditions are perfect here for these two species and during the summer months you will rarely see a more splendid display. Another introduced species appearing in September and October is the lovely pink Belladonna

Belladonna Lily

Lily (Amaryllis belladonna) which originates from South Africa, but which has naturalised well in Prazeres and appears in small clearings along this route. From here the water channel flows deeper into the forest looping around the mountain ridges occasionally giving views of the coastline and after 45 minutes reaches Ribeira Funda where a number of rocky pools have formed in the river bed. This is a pretty section of Levada Nova and also an easy route along the level levada path. There are no precipitous places either, so it is suitable for most ages and abilities. Another 30 minutes along we arrive at the Atalhinho Water House with its lovely garden area through which the levada passes. At this point a road drops down to the right passing the Atrio Guest House "Estralagem" and after a total of 700 mtrs, rejoins the ER222, making this an alternative option for anyone not wanting to cover the whole route.

However, continuing on from the Atalhinho Water House is so worthwhile as the further we go, the more picturesque the route becomes. The path again meanders through the woodland and within minutes passes between an old farm building and an orchard followed soon after by a fertile grazing area. Another few

minutes walking we then pass through a cattle gate and from here the scenery opens up allowing magnificent views of the slopes of the Paúl da Serra plateau. Along this second section wild Fuchsia grow beside the path and the valleys now become so deep that at times we are almost level with the tops of the eucalyptus trees growing from the slopes below. A little further along we reach Ribeira da Ached providing a picturesque place to stop for a rest. Here the river is hemmed in by craggy mountain slopes covered in

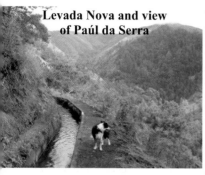

Levada Nova and view of Paúl da Serra

bracken and heaths which in autumn become multicoloured as the vegetation changes to shades of red, gold and brown; it's beautiful and at this valley head, the river tumbles down a lovely waterfall forming a number of large crystal pools at its base. After resting here, we continue to walk around two more isolated valleys high above Estrela da Calheta which are densely forested with only an occasional view of the coast to the south. From here mixed woodland takes over with species of Laurel, Oak, Sweet Chestnut and Mimosa to be found, the latter at its most magnificent in spring when its beautiful blossom fills the air with an amazing scent. Eventually the levada passes a small reservoir providing drinking water for Calheta, before crossing the ER211 which comes down from Rabaçal on Paul da Serra and leads on into Calheta. At this point leave the levada and turn right following the road, which now makes a 300 metre descent through a rich farming area with orchards and orange groves and many typical agricultural houses. The road eventually brings us into the centre of Estrela da Calheta where taxis are available, or alternatively the No. 107 or 80 buses running between Prazeres and Funchal, are routed through Estrela.

Walk 4   Prazeres Village to Paúl do Mar and Jardim do Mar

Walking time:
2hrs from Prazeres to Jardim do Mar via Paúl do Mar. Optional additional section from Jardim do Mar to Prazeres allow 1 hour minimum

Grade:
A strenuous and demanding walk with a steep descent of 500 m. There are no sheer drops but those walking this route should be sure footed and have a good head for heights. A further 3 km stretch is along a rocky coastal route which can be difficult underfoot. (Optional continuation of the walk to return to Prazeres from Jardim do Mar requires an ascent of 400 m up a steep and narrow path with a further 100m ascent along a cobbled road).

Directions and Starting Point:
Follow the R101 west to the roundabout in Prazeres and take the second turnoff signed Lombo da Rocha. At the end of the slip road, turn left and continue for approx 1 km to reach the overspill car park for the Jardim Atlántico Hotel or park next to the Vista Prazer restaurant and bar..

This is a truly memorable walk incorporating a challenging descent down an historic cobbled path, being the original municipal pathway connecting Paúl do Mar and Prazeres. The route takes us down to the harbour of this quaint fishing village as well as to the charming agricultural village of Jardim do Mar. Only by undertaking this walk can one imagine the difficulties

View from Prazeres

and isolation for the inhabitants of these two ancient villages, whose only alternative egress and access prior to the construction of roads in the 1960's, was by boat. The distance from Prazeres to Paúl is 1.8 kms with a descent of 500 m and thus the panoramic views en-route, are superb. This walk also incorporates one of the

very few coastal paths on the island; a 3 km stretch linking the two villages at sea level. There is also a final optional section, from Jardim do Mar to Prazeres, which results in a circular walk of perhaps 7 or 8 kms in total.

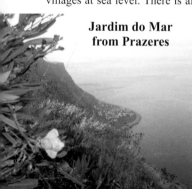

Jardim do Mar from Prazeres

There are a number of optional starting points for this walk, but I have chosen to start at the Vista Prazer restaurant and bar at Lombo da Rocha, from where the most exhilarating and spectacular section of this walk commences. From the bar descend down the road to the Jardim Atlántico Hotel continuing down the hotel driveway to a sign directing you to the "Caminho do Paúl do Mar" (meaning pathway). From here continue left following the driveway then take a right turn down a series of steps between two apartment blocks, where you will now find yourself at the cobbled path on the cliff tops. At this point you can take in wonderful views of the coastline with the villages of Paúl do Mar and Jardim do Mar nestling at the base of the cliffs. From here the route now starts to descend, at first on the wide cobbled path gradually zigzagging down between abandoned agricultural terraces, where a number of established Fig Trees still remain and after approximately 15 mins we reach a bench set beneath some Pine Trees; a lovely place to take a short rest. The remainder of the descent now follows an extremely steep gradient, so take your time, walking on such terrain can play havoc with your leg muscles and I

Prickly Pears

Historic cobbled path

would definitely recommend the use of walking poles for the whole of this walk. From here the route is quite awesome, with a landscape of ochre coloured volcanic cliffs, caves, waterfalls, indigenous plants and flowers and incredible views down to the harbour at Paúl do Mar. The vegetation along these cliffs is reasonably sparse although there are thickets of bushes including such species as the Globe Flower (Globularia salicina) and Prickly Pear (Opuntia tuna) as well as endemic species including Pride of Madeira (Echium nervosum), Viscid Houseleek (Aeonium glutinosum) and Fish Stunning Spurge (Euphorbia piscatoria). This latter plant has bluish-green leaves and a thick grey stems, which if broken excrete a poisonous milky fluid, which in former times was used by the

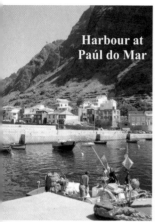

Harbour at Paúl do Mar

fishermen to stun the fish. On the final section of the descent a great cleft in the cliffs allows fine views of the Seco and Cova rivers as they crash down into the basin below, which we eventually cross on a concrete bridge before the final descent into the bustling harbour at Paúl do Mar. Here you can rest or take refreshments in one of the bars above the harbour.

The route now follows a coastal path along to Jardim do Mar. However, you should not overlook the danger here and always check the tide times

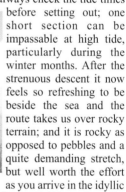

Coastal Path to Jardim do Mar

before setting out; one short section can be impassable at high tide, particularly during the winter months. After the strenuous descent it now feels so refreshing to be beside the sea and the route takes us over rocky terrain; and it is rocky as opposed to pebbles and a quite demanding stretch, but well worth the effort as you arrive in the idyllic village of Jardim do Mar. This village sits on a Fajá(meaning a flat plateau set between the ocean and mountainous cliffs) where the houses, with their colourful gardens, are clustered together along narrow mosaic pathways amongst banana plantations and vineyards; as its name suggests, it really is a "garden by the sea". Being an agricultural village, it also produces mangoes, avocados, papaya, custard apples and sweet potatoes to name just a few; it's a charming place preserving an ambience of quiet and calm from a bygone age. Leaving the beach ascend gently onto the new promenade which skirts the village and just before the Portinha (small harbour), take a left turn ascending a mosaic road which will lead you up to the village square, complete with its newly planted trees and fountains. I chose to end the walk here rather than cover the final strenuous section back to Prazeres. And so for those like me not wishing to continue, I suggest you call into the hotel in the village square, where you can arrange for a taxi to take you back to the starting point. Alternatively, those with surplus energy can now continue the walk on another historic trail up the

Village square

mountainside. In the centre of the village, just above Joe's Bar you will find a sign directing you right to Prazeres. Follow the path and steps which ascend up through the plantations and agricultural terraces soon arriving at a barbecue area and Mirodouro with fine view of the coastline and villages. From hereon the path becomes narrower and steeper as it climbs the rugged cliffs for a total of 400 m before arriving at a house on the cliff tops. In rainy weather the path can be quite wet and slippery; nevertheless it is a well used route by walking groups and individuals. From here a cobbled road now ascends another 100 mtrs to bring you on to a tarred road in Prazeres. Turn left here and continue for 0.6 km back to your starting point. Personally I am not convinced that this final section adds value to this otherwise spectacular and exhilarating walk, however those wanting a real challenge might disagree, but don't attempt to do this circular route in reverse, as to descend from Prazeres to Jardim do Mar can be quite difficult. Whichever route you chose, at the end of this walk you will definitely be ready for a long cold drink and I suggest you pop into Vista Prazer, a predominantly English speaking bar, where you are guaranteed a friendly welcome by the proprietors Jeff and Anna Binns.

Walk 5 Levada Nova – Loreto, Arco da Calheta to Canhas, Ponta do Sol

Walking time:
2hrs along a level levada path plus 30 mins descent to Canhas

Grade:
The path is mostly level and easy although there are a few challenging sections along the concrete shoulder of the levada which are exposed in places. Care is needed at these points. There is a final descent of around 300 mtrs down the ER209 at the end of the walk.

Directions and Starting Point:
From the roundabout on the new R101 before the Calheta tunnel take the first right signed Arco da Calheta. At the second roundabout take the second right which climbs to Loreto village. At the T-Junction with the ER222 turn left and as you leave the village take a right turn signed Paúl da Serra. The road climbs up through a residential area for 1.3 kms where the levada passes between two water tanks and a new industrial park on the left. Park at this point. The walk starts on the right beside a well, following the levada downstream.

It was a beautiful sunny day in late May as I left Loreto village to walk the final 8 km stretch of Levada Nova and what a marvellous

Valerian along levada

and varied route this turned out to be. The aqueduct flows through some spectacular scenery and I have yet to find a walk with so much colour as a result of the profusion of wild flowers that grow in this sunny southern location. But then again, Ponta do Sol does mean "sunny point" so what else would you expect.

The walk starts just above the cultivated land skirting the southern edge of the pine and eucalyptus forest at around 620 mtrs above sea level. Along the first stretch there are wonderful views down

the depression of Arco da Calheta and the coast beyond and the magnificent flora will not fail to impress anyone. Wild Valerian in shades of red, pink and white covered the slopes on either side of the channel in addition to blue and yellow vetch, purple and pink bindweed, yellow flowering broom and

Arco da Calheta

orange and yellow nasturtium, it was spectacular. After ten minutes the levada passes a small water house and regulation point before crossing over a cobbled road which leads to Pinheiro higher up the ridge. Along the next 100 mtr stretch the channel is then covered with concrete slabs forming stepping stones over the levada, some of which are broken, so care is needed crossing this section. Continuing on, the levada now passes through mixed woodland before sweeping into the deep valley of Ribeira Madalena from where the indigenous forest takes over and lovely views of Paúl da Serra come into sight. Around the whole of this magnificent valley, the levada flows between the rock face and the deep forested slopes and en-route passes through an eighteen metre tunnel (no need for a torch) which exits close to a small lake beside the rock through which the levada flows. From hereon the vegetation is lush due to the damp conditions and a spectacular

Levada Nova

plant you could not fail to miss is the endemic Disc Houseleek (Aeonium glandulosum) growing along the damp rock walls around the whole of the valley. This plant has a single leaf rosette, like a saucer, which grows to around 20 cms and clings to the basalt crevices; its leaves changing from green to pink in summer; a magnificent species. Continuing on we now pass a curious track descending sharp right into the deep valley. Ignore this and carry on into the first side valley where, in this totally isolated location, you will be amazed to see the hamlet of Pinheira on the hillside above and the tiny hamlet of Pomar lying on the route of the levada. It is difficult to imagine that these small communities could have existed here before access roads were created, obviously the track we passed a few minutes earlier was originally a lifeline for trade and amenities in the larger communities along the coast.

Now as you continue along the path you will hear the sound of the Ribeira do Pico da Urze, a tributary of the Madalena River, as it crashes down into the main valley. Just before the river the path is diverted down a series of steps on the right taking you over a bridge and leading you back up to the levada on another series of steps. In no way should you go along the levada shoulder at this point, it is impassable. I made that mistake and I must admit it was rather hairy. On the other side of the detour you now find yourself in Pomar; this tiny farming hamlet is perhaps no longer inhabited but nevertheless the terraces still appear to be cultivated and Fig and Walnut Trees grow beside the path. Along this stretch you will also see the Passion Flower vine (Passiflora) climbing over host trees, this is a species known locally as the Maracujá Banana due to the shape of its fruit; its large pink flower heads are really beautiful but unfortunately this invasive plant is rapidly becoming a threat to the natural forest. From here the levada flows around the main Madalena valley crossing the river on a high stepping stone bridge where lovely ferns grow in the deep rocky bed below. There is now another section where the parapet is narrow before a long stretch where the channel has been culverted and from here the forest begins to thin out allowing fine views south to Madalena and, looking back towards the hamlets, we can now see the high waterfall of Ribeira do Pica da Urze as it crashes into the

Passion Flower

Canary Dragon Herb

valley. Again many wild plants were in flower along this stretch including Large-leaved Saint John's Wort, Wild Roses, Violets and the lovely Canary Dragon Herb and there were also many butterflies around; I spotted the Speckled Wood and Red Admiral at this point. Leaving the valley we now turn east and eventually pass between agricultural plots and a nursery as we approach a tarred road at Eiras. After crossing the road we ascend a few steps to pick up the levada on the other side and continue on through an inhabited agricultural area crossing a number of concrete access roads and another small river. The path dips in and out of the forest which is now taken over by Pine and Eucalyptus and finally there are wonderful panoramic sea views before we arrive at Barreiro on the ER209, the regional road descending from Paúl da Serra. At this point turn right following the road for 0.6 km to a crossroad and continue straight ahead, signed Funchal, descending another 1.5 kms to meet the ER222 in Canhas. Turn left here to where taxis are available in the village centre to take you back to your starting point. Alternatively, if you prefer not to make the final descent, a taxi will collect you from the end of the levada at Barreiro.

Disc Houseleek

Walk 6   Lombada da Ponta do Sol – Levada Nova & Levada Moinha

Walking Time:-

Circular route - allow 3 hours

Grade:-

There is an initial 80 mtrs ascent from Solar dos Esmeraldos Manor house to Levada Nova. The paths along both levadas are level, however the shoulder of the Levada Nova requires good balance and a good head for heights. There are many long and extremely precipitous sections with no protection, so great care is essential and anyone suffering from vertigo should in no way attempt to walk along this higher channel. (See suggested alternative route). An 80 mtr descent takes you down to Levada Moinha. Obviously good footwear is essential as is a torch for the short tunnel and waterproofs for the waterfall

Directions and Starting Point:-

Follow the R101 highway west from Ribeira Brava. At the Ponta do Sol Shopping Centre roundabout take the first right up hill passing the secondary school on the left to a T-junction where the road meets the ER222. Turning right here, follow the road east for just over 1 km then take a left turn signed Lombada da Ponta do Sol. The road twists and climbs for just over 1 km passing the snack bar La Babariaon the left. As you continue along this road the Mansion House of Solar dos Esmeraldos and Espirito Santo Chapel become clearly visible higher up the ridge, this is your destination. A little further along take a sharp left which brings you into the square beside the chapel. Parking is available at this point.

This is a wonderful day out and a must for anyone who enjoys the natural and built environment as well as those who can't resist a slightly more challenging walk. Lombada da Ponta do Sol is situated at a height of 320 mtrs on a mountain ridge running along the eastern side of the Ponta do Sol valley. The walk starts from the ancient Solar dos Esmeraldos Mansion

Solar dos Esmeraldos

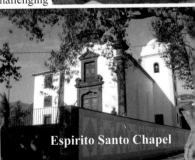
Espirito Santo Chapel

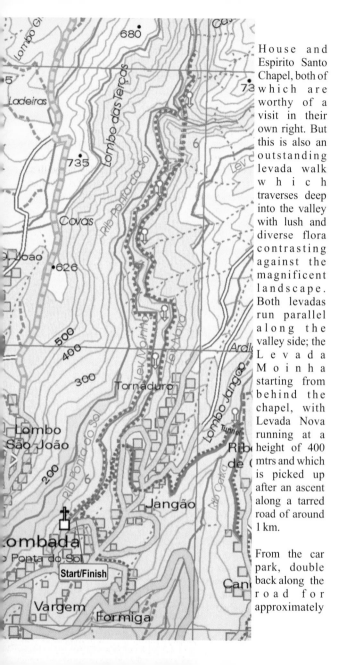

House and Espirito Santo Chapel, both of which are worthy of a visit in their own right. But this is also an outstanding levada walk which traverses deep into the valley with lush and diverse flora contrasting against the magnificent landscape. Both levadas run parallel along the valley side; the Levada Moinha starting from behind the chapel, with Levada Nova running at a height of 400 mtrs and which is picked up after an ascent along a tarred road of around 1 km.

From the car park, double back along the road for approximately

100 mtrs, taking a left turn which climbs to the hamlet of Jangão. At a bend in the road before the hamlet, a series of steps climb up between the houses and the levada crosses the path under a section of paving stones between the buildings. Follow the levada upstream leaving the hamlet behind and passing through sugar cane plantations and agricultural terraces. From this point the views of the distant mountain range are in view and you will find yourself looking up towards Cascalha and Bica da Cana on Paúl da Serra. I walked along this route in April with my friends Anna and Jeff Binns from Prazeres and we had a wonderful day out with a picnic en-route. The vegetation along the whole of this circular walk is fantastic, with so many wild flowers and plants providing an abundance of colour and shape. The water channel clings to the valley side and in places is carved into the rock, which overhangs allowing water to trickle down into the levada; the habitat for many ferns, mosses and Liverworts as well as the endemic Disc House-Leek (Aeonium glandulosum). The Shrubby Sow Thistle (Sonches fruticosus), better described as the Giant Dandelion Tree, also grows in crevices along the levada here. This plant is another endemic to Madeira and is one of my favourites due to its size. It grows up to 4 mtrs with a thick trunk and bright yellow inflorescences which are instantly recognisable as the dandelion family.

The path meanders in and out of short side valleys as it progresses into the natural forest and after 50 minutes you reach a tunnel which is around 200mtrs long and has been carved through the rock. The headroom at the entrance is quite low, but the tunnel is dry underfoot and you can see the other end as you enter, nevertheless a torch is required. The exit from the tunnel is the most exciting bit as you come face to face with a spectacular waterfall as it crashes down a rocky chasm into the valley below. At this point the levada passes behind the waterfall, hence the need for a waterproof. Also of interest here, is the point below where the water collects. You look down onto a canopy of Willows and Poplars and when I

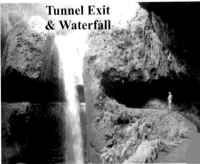

Tunnel Exit & Waterfall

Levada Moinha

visited in April it was a mass of yellow flowering Greater Celandine (Chelidonium majus) a species of the poppy family indigenous to the Laurel forests in Madeira. After walking a further fifteen minutes along the path you will reach the Ponta do Sol river bed and the source of

Levada Moinha

the levada. This is an ideal location to stop for a picnic and admire the beauty all around. From here retrace your steps back towards the waterfall for a few minutes and then on a bend just after you cross a water diversion channel, you will see a narrow sandy path descending to the right; this is the route down to Levada Moinha. This levada has recently been rebuilt with protective fencing erected on most of the dangerous sections. Now follow the channel downstream until

Restored Corn Mill

eventually the chapel of Espirito Santo again comes into view. Along this path you will pass Fig Trees (Ficus carica) and Loquat Trees (Eriobotrya japonica) which have naturalised here. The path eventually brings you round the back of the chapel to Solar dos Esmeraldos. In the past, the aqueduct Moinha fed a sugar cane mill and the grinding wheel of a corn flour mill from which it takes its name (Moinha meaning mill). The latter still stands close to the chapel and has been restored within a lovely little garden. The chute which directed the water into the mill, still exists and it is possible to climb a short flight of steps to peer down inside.

An alternative, for those lacking a head for heights, is to walk along Levada Moinha in both directions thus avoiding the more dangerous path of the Levada Nova. The ascent from the source of this levada is quite steep but it's well worth the climb to get to the magnificent waterfall and the lovely area of the riverbed.

The Solar dos Esmeraldos Estate
The striking Manor House of Solar dos Esmeraldos, painted in a traditional rose colour, was built by Joáo Esmeraldo over 500 years ago. Esmeraldo arrived in Madeira in 1480, a Flemish merchant who was the first sugar baron to settle in Madeira and was reputed to be a friend of Christopher Columbus. He bought the land at the end of the fifteenth century from the two sons of João Gonçalves Zarco, the Portuguese Captain who discovered Madeira and landed here in 1420. The sugar production of this vast estate was carried out by slaves who worked the land and provided the wealth for Esmeraldo to construct this enormous country home. Esmeraldo's main residence was in Funchal, known as Columbus's House, but this was unfortunately demolished in 1876. However, the Museu do Açúcar in Praça de Colombo, Funchal, provides good documentation for anyone interested. Over the years the house has been extensively modified and in the recent past has been restored and is now used as the village school. At some point in the intervening years it was also used as a Convent.

Around the same time Esmeraldo also commissioned the construction of the Espirito Santo Chapel adjacent to the house. This was rebuilt in the 18th century and is a lovely example of Portuguese religious architecture. In addition to its extremely ornate interior with rich baroque carvings, there are many wonderful Azulejos (the traditional blue and white glazed tiles) which are set around the lower walls of the nave and chancel.

Both these historic buildings and the former corn mill are well worth a visit. The corn mill is open weekdays between 9.00 a.m. and 5.00 p.m. and the church is open on Saturday evening at 5.00 p.m as well as for Sunday Services.

Walk 7   The Tunnel and Trail to 25 Fontes

Walking time:
2hrs 40mins return.

Grade:
Easy walking, mostly along level paths. There are some narrow sections along the levada shoulder and some precipitous places. Care should be taken at these points. There is an 800 metre tunnel to negotiate in both directions but it is dry, has plenty of head room and is good underfoot. A torch is essential.

Directions and Starting Point:
From Ribeira Brava follow the ER104 (São Vicente) then take the ER228 Serra de Água to Encumeada Pass. From here go left onto the ER110 to the new cross roads on Paúl da Serra. Drive straight ahead for a further 4.5 kms passing the Rabaçal car park on the right to where the ER211 turns off left signed Calheta. Drive 2 kms down the hill to a newly erected Forestry picnic shelter standing on a sharp bend. Alternatively approach from Estrela da Calheta via the new highway R101. Parking is available at this point.

Most people intending walking Levada das 25 Fontes will no doubt find themselves at a car park above Rabaçal on the ER110, 1340 mtrs above sea level. This valley is one of the most beautiful on the island and one most frequented by walkers. It lies on the western slopes of the Paúl da Serra plateau on the northern half of the central mountain range and is located 4 kms west of the new cross roads at Paúl da Serra. The car park is a starting point for a number of wonderful walks, not only into the interior of Rabaçal valley, to Levada das 25 Fontes, Levada do Risco, Levada da Rocha Vermelha and Lagoa do Vento, but also for a wonderful

Reservoir & Chapel

walk into the Ribeira Grande Valley culminating in a magnificent waterfall and trout pool. Also by crossing over the ER110 and passing in front of the reservoir and the chapel of Nossa Sra de Fátima, one can walk Levada do Paúl along the southern slopes to the Cristo Rei statue on the ER209.

Nevertheless for the purpose of this walk let us concentrate on a journey to 25 Fontes, a return distance of 8 miles from the car park with a descent of c.380 mtrs. The levada is approached via a winding road leading down to Rabaçal Posto Florestal and from there down a series of steps on a wooded slope until you reach Levada das 25 Fontes. The route is well signed and the descent is the easy bit, but making the ascent back at the end of a hot day and after much walking, can be a little less so. However at this point, I will let you into a secret, there is a wonderful alternative route via the Calheta tunnel which makes for a more interesting, exciting and almost level walk. The route is comfortable most of the way and is suitable for most abilities. In fact I took my grandchildren along here last spring and they thought it was "cool" (modern speak of course).

Descent to Rabaçal

From the Rabaçal car park drive a further half a kilometre west to the ER211, a left turn signed Calheta. Drive 2 kms down the hill to a Forestry picnic shelter standing on a sharp bend. Notice the change in landscape as you descend this road changing from rolling moorland, with heather and gorse, to Pine and Eucalyptus

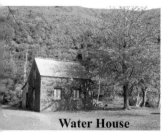

Water House

forest a little lower down. There are usually a number of minibuses parked at this spot during the day so it's easy to find. From here a wide track leads off to the left into the forest. Follow this for 10 mins into the next valley whereupon you reach a small Water House at the valley head. The tunnel entrance is just behind this building and the wide entrance is covered in ferns and trickling water. The tunnel is around 800 mtrs long and takes 15 – 20 minutes to negotiate. You will definitely need a torch and possibly a sweater depending on the weather but the interior is clean and dry except for an occasional puddle on the path, and there is good head room.

Northern Entrance Rabaçal Tunnel

On emerging from the tunnel you will come face to face with the lush vegetation of the island's interior Heath Forests. Also take note of a little shrine at the tunnel exit where you emerge onto a flat platform. From here the direction is clear and you will immediately cross the Ribeira do Alecrim gorge. Now follow the Levada das 25 Fontes upstream for 55 minutes until you reach your destination. After 20 mins you pass steps leading up to the Rabaçal Posto Florestal and Levada do Risco. A further 5 mins along you cross a bridge over the deep gorge of Ribeira Grande and soon after descend a series of steps leaving the levada for a short time before ascending another set of steps to a small water house where you again pick up the levada. From here the path

Levada das 25 Fontes

becomes narrower with some precipitous drops but these are mostly protected. However, the levada at this point runs along a 2ft parapet providing a natural hand rail along this section. Along the whole route gaps in the vegetation allow magnificent views down the Ribeira da Janela Valley. The vegetation is dominated by Ancient Tree Heaths,

Madeiran Bilberry and Laurel and along the route many of these trees are draped in lichen and mosses. In summer the array of flowers is superb with the endemic Madeira Moneywort (Sibthorpia peregrina) with its little yellow flower, growing in profusion along the levada's edge. You can also see the Chrysanthemum Shrub (Asteraceae), Crane's Bill (Geraniaceae) and once again the Shrubby Sow Thistle (Sonchus fruticosus) growing in the moist ravines. These huge dandelion trees are a real phenomenon. Coming from England most will agree that the dandelion is much maligned and regarded as a weed. These here are magnificent. Arriving at 25 Fontes you now walk into an amphitheatre where water cascades down into pools in a rock basin and you can scramble over the large boulders in an area green with ferns and other vegetation. As a further option the levada can also be followed for a further 10 minutes taking you to its source.

25 Fontes

Return is by the same route, and once back through the tunnel on the Calheta side you should take time to admire the wonderful views down the Calheta slopes. In the distance you will see Levada da Rocha Vermelha which has also been channelled through a tunnel at a lower level and also the Levada Nova further down still. Both these channels, as well as the Levada das 25 Fontes feed the Calheta Hydropower Station and also provide essential water for irrigation on the south coast. From this point it is also possible to walk down the valley into Estrela da Calheta and to Laureate in Arc, but perhaps this should be left for another day.

Walking Time:
Approximately 2 hours from Rabaçal car park return. Alternative route also 2 hours via the tunnel to the Forestry picnic shelter on the ER211.

Grade:
An easy descent down a tarred road and thereafter on a broad levada path. The route is signposted and precipitous places at Risco Waterfall are mostly protected. The return, by the same route, necessitates a 250 mtr ascent back to the car park. The alternative route, terminating on the Calheta slopes, entails a further 100 metre descent and negotiates an 800 metre tunnel for which a torch is essential.

Directions and Starting Point:
From Ribeira Brava follow the ER104 (São Vicente) then take the ER228 Serra de Água to Encumeada Pass (11 kms). At Encumeada go left on the ER110 to the new cross roads on Paúl da Serra. (14kms). Drive straight ahead for a further 4 kms passing the Jungle Rain Restaurant on the right. The car park is on the right.

From Estrela da Calheta hospital, follow the signs for Rabaçal ER211. Continue up hill for 6 kms to meet the Paúl da Serra road ER110. Turn right. Rabaçal car park is just under 1 km on the left. (Note: you will pass the new Forestry picnic site on your ascent up the ER21l)

The walk to this impressive waterfall is a must for anyone wanting to discover Madeira's interior. At Risco Waterfall, the Ribeira Grande plunges 100 mtrs down a sheer rock face from Lagoa do Vento then falling a further 100 mtrs down to Levada das 25 Fontes before continuing on into the Ribeira da Janela Valley in the north west. The route to this beauty spot is well trodden and a favourite amongst visitors to the island and the walk starts at Rabaçal car park on the western slopes of the Paúl da Serra plateau. From the road barrier on the right of the car park, descend down the tarred road to the Rabaçal Posto Florestal, which can be seen from the car park nestling in the Heath Forests in the valley below. As we descend the road twists and bends around the valley head eventually crossing Ribeira do Alecrim which flows from Paúl da Serra. The vegetation at this altitude is dominated by Ancient Heaths, which are interspersed with Madeira Bilberry,

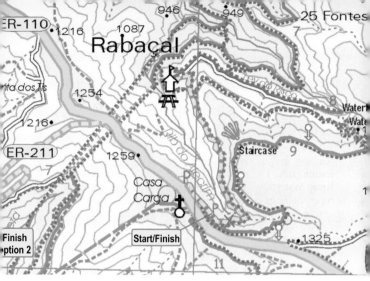

Canary Island Laurel and Madeira Mahogany and which together provide reasonably low, yet extremely dense forest.

The walk to the Forestry House takes approximately 25 minutes and as we approach the rear of the building a sign for Risco Waterfall and 25 Fontes appears. From here we take a right turn descending on a stony path through the shady woodland soon picking up Levada do Risco. After 10 minutes another sign directs the route to Levada das 25 Fontes, but ignore this and continue to follow the levada upstream. The damp habitat along this channel supports numerous varieties of ferns, mosses and grasses and if walking here in spring or summer you can expect to see a number of endemic and indigenous flora including the Shrubby Sow Thistle, Anemone-Leaved Crane's Bill (Geranium), Madeira Orchid, Canary Buttercup and Madeira Moneywort as well as many other species. The vistas along this section offer beautiful views down the Ribeira da Janela valley with Levada das 25 Fontes and Levada da Rocha Vermelha clearly visible in the valley below.

Fifteen minutes after the sign you arrive in the semicircular basin of Risco

Risco Waterfall

Waterfall and from the viewpoint you can admire this spectacular natural landmark. The waterfall crashes down the volcanic rock face disappearing from view into the valley far below. From this point the levada path is no longer passable but can be seen as it tunnels into the rock leading behind the waterfall and then on through further tunnels around the basin and on through the wooded rock face leading north. I walked this route in December, and due to the unusually heavy rainfall, it was quite spectacular. On my previous visit in summer there was much less water; nevertheless it was still very impressive.

Returning from Risco, you now have a number of options. You can either retrace your steps eventually ascending the road back to the car park, or alternatively you can continue on to 25 Fontes or into the Calheta valley. For these last two options you need to return to the signpost for 25 Fontes which now leads off to the right down a stone laid path which drops steadily through

Alternative Route

the woodland and eventually brings you to a T-Junction on the path beside Levada das 25 Fontes. Turning right here leads directly on to the famous beauty spot (Refer Walk 7 – Tunnel and Trail to 25 Fontes). Turning left at the junction follows the levada downstream eventually bringing you to the Calheta tunnel through which you approach the Water House and irrigation system providing water for the Calheta Hydropower Station in

Steps to Levada das 25 Fontes

the south. The tunnel is 800 metres long and takes around 15 – 20 minutes to negotiate. You definitely need a torch but the interior is safe, dry and clean and it has good headroom. On emerging from the tunnel you will become immediately aware of both the changes in temperature and in the vegetation, as you now face the south coast. This is a lovely spot and from here you follow a wide track for 10 minutes to lead you back to the ER211. The younger and fitter amongst you will have no difficulty ascending the 2 kms of road back to Rabaçal. However personally, I prefer to walk on level or downhill

Levada das 25 Fontes

terrain and so a friend and I took two cars leaving one at the new Forestry picnic site on the ER211 for our eventual return to Rabaçal. On my previous visit I hired a taxi from Estrela da Calheta and dropped my car en-route, continuing on by taxi to Rabaçal. The charge was around €15.

Tunnel Entrance

Walk 9 The Ribeira Grande Valley – Rabaçal

Walking Time:
Total time approximately 2 hours return.

Grade:
An easy grade walk along the levada shoulder but slightly stony underfoot along the first section. There are one or two mildly precipitous places along the route, however the path is wide and the thick vegetation provides protection. This walk is suitable for most abilities.

Directions and Starting Point:
Follow directions for Walk 8 to Rabaçal car park

The Ribeira Grande flows from the highlands of Paúl da Serra and is one of the source rivers of Ribeira da Janela flowing below Rabaçal to the north coast. At the end of this lovely walk you arrive at a spectacular gorge with an impressive waterfall and mountain pool where you can enjoy a swim, relax with a picnic or just feed the trout. This is yet another favourite with visitors to the island and the walk starts from the Rabaçal car park on the ER 110 lying on the western slopes of the Paúl da Serra plateau. Looking NE from the car park the route to Ribeira Grande can be seen as an almost straight line through the heath forests as it maintains height

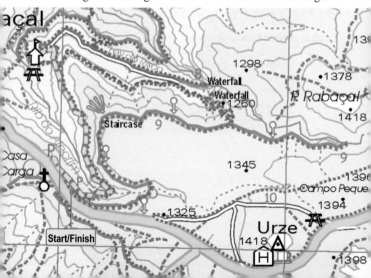

along the contours of the hillside.

From the car park follow the tarred road to the right for approximately 100 mtrs to a road barrier at which point a well trodden path leads off to the right, which we now follow for a further 50 mtrs to reach Levada do Paúl. The levada flows under

Levada do Paúl

the ER110 at this point, but we turn left to follow it upstream taking care along this first stretch which is quite stony underfoot but which soon improves as you progress along. The levada flows between the rocky hillside and the dense vegetation of the Heath Forest which forms the natural transition between the Laurisilva and the higher mountain peaks.

The vegetation at this altitude consists largely of Ancient Heath trees interspersed with Giant Madeira Bilberry and the occasional Canary Island Laurel. The path winds around the hillside and after 10 minutes reaches Ribeira do Alecrim where you will find a water tank and trout pond. From here the path follows a wide left hand bend as it negotiates the valley head continuing along the southern flank of Pico Rabaçal. Continuing along the path from here there are now a few slightly precipitous places but it is quite safe and the path is good and reasonably wide with the lush vegetation giving a sense of security. At approximately the half way point we now

reach an impressive water stairway where the levada rushes down a channel from its higher level and once at the top we are rewarded with magnificent views down the Rabaçal valley and further down towards Ribeira da Janela and the north coast. From here you can also see the course of the Levada dos 25 Fontes and Levada da Rocha Vermelha as they snake their way through the lower vegetation in the valley below. From here continue along the levada path

Water Stairway

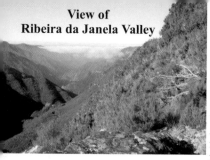

View of Ribeira da Janela Valley

taking in views of the gentle rolling hilltops which rise above the tree line and which change colour dramatically with the changing seasons. After approximately 25 minutes we eventually reach the source of the levada at the deep gorge and river bed of the Ribeira Grande which cascades down from Pico Rabaçal. Looking below the path as you approach the river, you will also see Lagoa do Vento lower down the gorge; this is a tiny lake surrounded by cliffs formed by the onward flow of the river and can be accessed by an alternative route from the Rabaçal Forestry Post.

However, for the purpose of this walk, we now return from here by the same route but definitely not before enjoying this idyllic location. Here you can scramble over the rocky river bed with its large boulders to find a wonderful rock pool where you can rest, take a picnic or even a swim if the weather is warm, but be warned, the water is exceptionally cold during the winter months. I can vouch for this as on a previous visit, my family took their wet suits and enjoyed a quick dip to the great amusement of other visitors around. Nevertheless whatever the weather, be sure to take along a little extra food to feed the numerous trout that dash around the pool and which give lots of amusement as they fight and jostle for tit bits.

For the more energetic it should also be noted that from this destination it is possible to climb above the waterfall and following the river bed over Pico Rabaçal to eventually link with

Ribeira Grande Waterfall

Walk 10, a circular route from Lajeado to Jungle Rain Restaurant at Pico de Urze on the ER110. This provides a lovely mixture of forest, moorland and levada walking with a duration of approximately three to four hours.

Walk 10   Off the beaten track
in Paúl da Serra

Walking time:
1 hr 45 mins circular route.
Grade:-
Easy walking, mostly along good surfaces but with an occasional boulder which slightly obstructs the path. Some reasonably deep drops along the route which are unprotected but the thick vegetation provides security therefore little danger. The initial descent and ascents towards the end of the walk, are negligible.
Directions and Starting Point:-
From the new cross roads on the ER110 at Paúl da Serra, take the road signed Fanal & Ribeira da Janela for approximately 200 mtrs to the junction with the Fanal road. Here continue left on the old ER110 for half a kilometre until you see a sign on the right for Lajeado. A short tarred road leads into a grassy car park. You are at a height of 1398 mtrs; the walk starts at this point.

From the car park go directly ahead over the brink of the hill continuing into the valley below along a clear broad path which descends left through the bracken down to the river bed. This is the Ribeira do Lajeado, a source river of the Ribeira Grande, which winds its way down the western slopes of Paúl da Serra into the Rabaçal valley. On reaching the river you will cross a tiny stone bridge over a narrow levada just beyond its source. At this point you will be looking across at a rock face on the other side of the river which is covered in lush vegetation with tiny waterfalls cascading down from Pico Rabaçal above. Anyone familiar with the Yorkshire Dales will see a resemblance with this area, from the large rolling hills and stony river bed, to the familiar vegetation and even the presence of dry stone walling; probably livestock pens which are arranged in an array of strange patterns. (The continuation of walk 9 from Ribeira Grande, links at this point)

The route now follows the levada downstream along a clear path which meanders around the valley, roughly parallel to the ER110 road above and with the Ribeira do Lajeado dropping away from you to the right. At this point you are on the edge of the Heath Forests which continue into the Rabaçal valley. The whole of the walk is dominated by the Ancient Tree Heath, Besom Heath and

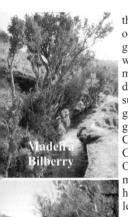
Madeira Bilberry

the water channel

the endemic Madeira Bilberry as well as the occasional Laurel. The path is also flanked by gorse, broom, bramble and bracken and many wild flowers appear during the summer months. The colours here change dramatically with the seasons. In summer the surrounding hillsides are covered in the olive green bracken, contrasted against the yellow gorse and broom. The wild flowers include Chrysanthemum, Herb Robert, Self Heal, Canary Buttercups, Violets and Madeira Orchids plus a rich variety of ferns and mosses. In winter the bracken dries off, the hills take on a copper glow and the Bilberry leaves turn a brilliant red, with the new shoots of the Heaths providing a lovely yellowish contrast. This levada, unlike most of the traditional irrigation channels across the island, appears to have evolved from a natural mountain stream with reinforced sections to contain the water flow. It is a wonderful secluded place which does not appear in any of the guide books and is not shown clearly on any maps, but a walk along this lovely stretch of moorland is rewarding. The whole area is

quiet, remote and peaceful, passing through vegetation which often forms a canopy over the path. The stream or levada is crystal clear with trout dashing around in the water.

Pico Rabaçal

After 20 minutes, the path follows round into a side valley and soon crosses another river with large waterfalls pouring into the rocky river bed. Here the path fords the river over a concrete water course designed to direct spate water away from the levada. Around this valley head smaller waterfalls cascade into the levada building up the momentum in its flow west. Along most of the route the Ancient Heaths are draped in lichens and beard moss and many have knarled and coiled trunks which have formed into magnificent wild sculptures. The Heath trees provide a habitat for the Madeiran Firecrest (Regulus Ignicapillus madeirensis) which flit about the branches and were very visible and audible on my visit there in January. A little further along you cross a style and from this point the vegetation opens up in places giving magnificent views down the Rabaçal valley. From this point the terrain changes into lower shrub land and in summer you will often find cattle grazing along this stretch. This is not a problem as there are a number of flat slabs enabling you to cross to the opposite side of the levada if you wish to, whilst you pass. A few more metres along the levada comes to an abrupt end where the water gushes down into Ribeira do Alecrim, which again flows down to Rabaçal. From here you follow a path to the right through the bracken until you

Moorland View

reach a rickety bridge a little lower down the river. Although I say rickety, it is safe, but alternatively you can ford the river at this point. On the far side a wide gravel path leads up a small hillside and eventually widens out into a number of tracks all of which lead up the ER110 close to an old stone barn.

Nossa Sra. de Fátima

From here turn left following the ER110 east. After 0.8 km you reach the Estralagem Pico da Urze and the Jungle Rain Restaurant and shop, where you can stop for refreshments. Worth attention at this point is the adjacent chapel, a shrine to Nossa Senhora de Fátima. It is really lovely, set into the rock face behind and erected at the time the hotel was built. It is well worth a visit.

The new section of the ER110 passes the hotel with the old road closed off to traffic a few metres ahead. Nevertheless it is still possible to walk the old road back to your starting point. It is around 1½ kms back to Lajeado car park. Along the old section of road you will pass a grove of conifers on the left at the head of the valley you passed over on the levada. These coniferous plantations appear frequently on the Paul da Serra plateau and are often cultivated around the Postos Florestais. They consist of Pine, Spruce, Cypress and Fir; the Douglas Fir (Pseudotsuga menziesii) being easily recognised by the distinct smell of oranges when you rub the needles. These plantations are out of character with the rest of the area; nevertheless they seem to provide an oasis in what could otherwise be described as an extremely barren landscape.

I have walked this route a number of times in all seasons but in the winter months the temperature at this altitude can get quite cold, so a warm jacket is recommended. In fact, on my visit in early January, as I walked in the sunshine, I was staggered to find ice patches along the path. Now that really did bring back memories of the Yorkshire Dales.

The Southern Slopes of Paúl da Serra

Walk 11 Cristo Rei along Levada da Bica da Cana
Walk 12 Cristo Rei to Fátima chapel – Rabaçal

Walking Times:
Walk 11- 1hr. 40 mins return - Walk 12 - 2 hr 30 mins return.
Grade:
Both routes provide for easy walking along narrow levada paths on the open moorland. There is a precipitous section towards the end of walk 11 where the shoulder of the channel is narrow and the rock wall overhangs. Care should be taken at this point.

Directions and Starting Point:
From Ribeira Brava follow the ER104 (São Vicente) then take the ER228 Serra de Água to Encumeada Pass (11 kms). At Encumeada go left on the ER110 to the new cross roads on Paúl da Serra. (14kms). Turn left taking the ER209 for 3 kms, Cristo Rei statue is on the right. From Canhas, above Ponta do Sol, follow the ER209 for 9kms to Cristo Rei. Parking is available by the statue or on the roadside.

The Cristo Rei statue stands prominently on the edge of the Paúl da Serra plateau looking down over the southern coastline to Ponta do Sol, 1300 mtrs below. This is an area of lovely open moorland dominated by bracken, heather and gorse providing a refreshing alternative to forest and woodland walking, being characteristic of many of Madeira's levada walks. On a clear day you will find the views breathtaking and both routes provide exhilarating walking whilst covering reasonably easy and comfortable terrain. The two levadas run east and west from the

Cristo Rei statue

ER 209 crossing approximately 100 mtrs down the road from the statue car park.

Walk 11 – Cristo Rei along Levada da Bica da Cana

Dropping down the road from the statue, Levada do Paúl crosses in front of a water house standing on the left. Taking the levada east in front of the house and passing through a rock cutting, the channels now separate and from here we follow Levada da Bica do Cana upstream as it winds its way around the hillsides occasionally crossing small becks and springs and as we stroll along we can take in the superb views to the south with the towns and villages scattered along the coast line. After 20 minutes we arrive at a picnic spot where a huge Pine tree stands in isolation and is

Huge Pine in isolation

quite magnificent, then a few metres further along the channel crosses a cobbled track leading down from Paúl da Serra to Ponta do Sol. On the opposite side of the track the levada can now be seen as it courses down a slope which we have to ascend to bring us to a viewpoint at the top of the slope. The path now leads in loops

Levada da Bica da Cana

around a steep and rugged valley and from hereon we leave all signs of habitation behind with the changing vistas providing spectacular views of the mountain range below Bica da Cana and the Encumeada Pass.

The route is beautiful and remote as we continue deeper into the valley, however towards the end of the walk there are a couple of exposed concrete sections of the levada shoulder which are also hampered by

**Mountain view from
Levada da Bica da Cana**

overhanging rock; nevertheless these short sections are quite passable with care and we soon continues on the grass and stone pathway bringing us to the end of this short walk at a point where we meet with a wide sandy track descending right. At this junction the Levada Bica do Cana is no longer passable as it continues around the valley side and can be seen making a steep descent from Bica da Cana. I have chosen this point as the final destination for this short walk and from here we retrace our steps back to Cristo Rei.

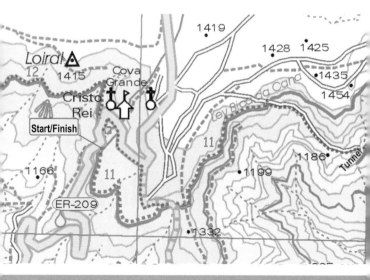

To continue on from here would requires a descent of 350 mtrs down the wide sandy track which would eventually bring you to Cascalha being the valley head and source of the Ponta do Sol river and where a number of waterfalls cascade down over rock-walled amphitheatres. If you choose to take this route you then have two alternatives; either to retrace your steps with the resultant 350 mtr climb back to Levada Bica da Cana and on to Cristo Rei, or to continue on to Encumeada, linking with Walk 15 of this series. For some reason this particular route fascinates me, but I will leave this for another day when I have lots of energy and a few intrepid souls to accompany me. However, as a matter of interest, the total distance to Encumeada is around 12 kms, takes approximately 5 hours and passes through three tunnels en-route, the longest of which is 2 kms and takes 1 hour to negotiate.

Walk 12   Cristo Rei to Fátima chapel - Rabaçal

South coast from Levada do Paúl

Starting on the opposite side of the ER209, follow Levada do Paul downstream. Again this is a very narrow levada channel, but due to its easy flow along the open moorland, there are no dangerous or difficult sections to negotiate and therefore this route makes for a lovely gentle ramble. On a clear day you will have wonderful views of the ocean and coastline far beyond the green expanse of the southern sloping hills. In spring and summer you will find ferns, heather and gorse and many wild flowers, whilst during the winter months the slopes turn to autumnal colours, each season providing its own contrasts. The route is well used so you will undoubtedly meet other walkers passing in each direction and it is also a grazing area, so occasionally you may meet with cattle along the path, but being well accustomed to walkers, they are not obstructive. At points the path crosses a number of streams with small waterfalls and eventually passes just below Pico da Urze Estralagem and Restaurant. A little further along the levada is channelled under the newly constructed Arco

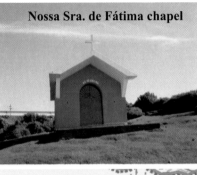

Nossa Sra. de Fátima chapel

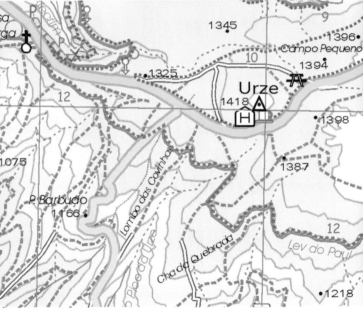

road which leads down from the ER 110. (Just as an aside, I suggest that you take a drive down this new access road on your return journey; due to the gradient, the views of the coast are amazing). Levada do Paúl covers around 5 kms and terminates at the pretty Nossa Senhora de Fátima chapel and the reservoir across from the Rabaçal miradouro and car park.. Once at Rabaçal you can either return the same way or follow the ER110 and ER 209 back to your starting point and perhaps call into the Jungle Rain Bar and Restaurant en-route for a rest and refreshments.

Cristo Rei Statue
The white marble statue of Cristo Rei was erected in 1962; it is also known as Nosso Senhor do Montanha (Our Lord of the Mountain). The area of Cristo Rei is surrounded by trees and terracing creating a little oasis in this lonely moorland area. Below the statue stands a large arch, other sculptures and a spring, plus a number of stone plinths inscribed with religious proverbs.

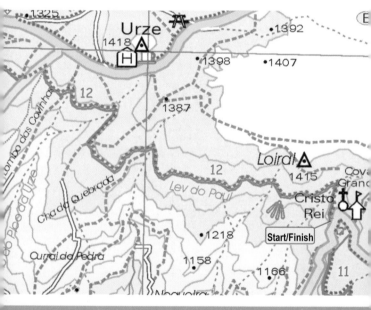

Walk 13 Bica da Cana to Pináculo
- Madeira´s Sugar Loaf Mountain

Walking Time:
Circular Route - Allow 2½ hours
Grade:
A reasonably easy ascent of 80 mtrs leads to a Miradouro and the
starting point, with any easy descent of c.160 mtrs to Levada da
Serra and Sugar Loaf Mountain. At this level there are good wide
paths with very few precipitous places but slightly slippery
sections at the base of the waterfalls, so care should be taken at
these points. Otherwise a level and easy route suitable for most
abilities. A further 80 mtrs ascent leads you back to the E110.
Directions and Starting Point:-
From the Rapido at Ribeira Brava follow the ER104 (São Vicente)
then take the ER228 Serra de Água to Encumeada Pass (11 kms).
At Encumeada go left on the ER110 for approximately 8 kms. The
Bica da Cana picnic site is on the right. Alternatively from Canhas
above Ponta do Sol, follow the ER209 for 12 kms to the new Paúl
da Serra cross roads. Turn right and continue for 4½ kms. Bica da

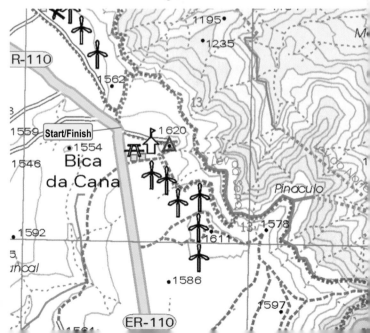

Cana is signed on the left. There is adequate parking either on the roadside or in the adjacent car park.

Bica da Cana lies on the north eastern edge of the Paúl da Serra plateau and this walk is located below the rocky cliffs overlooking the São Vicente valley. Bica da Cana is a popular weekend picnic and recreation site and close by the Forestry House you will find picnic tables, cooking and barbecue facilities and toilets.

I have christened this walk the "trail of the giant plants" as I find it fascinating that so many of the most common plants found in the

Madeira Orchid

English countryside grow to mammoth proportions in Madeira. This is obviously due to the sub-tropical climate and the volcanic soil, and on this particular walk, more than anywhere else I have seen on the island, these grow in abundance. There are numerous gigantic species of Dandelions, Buttercups, Thistles, Chrysanthemums, Bilberries and Heathers. Also at this time of year, it was June when I walked this route, these plants are interspersed with Madeira Orchids, Madeira Mountain Stocks, Violets and Stonecrops as well as carpets of large Anemone-Leaved Crane's-Bill, all providing a wonderful

Common Broom

array of colour. Many of these plants are species endemic to Madeira; I spotted at least a dozen of these on my recent visit, making this a really excellent location for those interested in discovering the island's unique flora. Additionally, large sections of the route were flanked with yellow flowering Broom, at their best in early summer, and these banks of colour were enhanced by the appearance of many species of butterfly. Pushing our way through this vegetation was like a take from Alice in Wonderland, it was so very wild and beautiful. This lush and varied flora provides an ideal habitat for Madeira Brimstone, Monarch and Speckled Wood butterflies with the Heaths providing a home for the beautifully coloured Chaffinches that flit within their branches. However, enough of me waxing lyrical; it's time we got on with the walk.

From the main gate and entrance to the Forestry House, follow a cobbled path and stairway up to the Miradouro and an additional picnic area. From here you can take in the spectacular views of Madeira's highest mountain peaks including Pico Ruivo and Pico Arieiro which are clearly visible from this point. Also looking down you will see the pathway leading to Pináculo peak in the valley below. My Brazilian friend Cláudia Nunes accompanied me on this walk. Cláudia lives in Jardim do Mar but her original home was Rio da Janeiro and she was interested in comparing Madeira's Sugar Loaf Mountain to Rio's. I have also visited Sugar Loaf in Rio, and we both agreed that whilst Pináculo is very similar in shape, that's where the likeness ends, it is tiny by comparison, basically a large outcrop of Basalt rock mostly covered with vegetation. Nevertheless it still forms an imposing sight set against the magnificent backdrop of the central massif. From the viewpoint follow a path which passes a picnic table and leads up to a trig point at the highest level (1620 mtrs) where two further paths descend down hill in the direction of the wind turbines. The path to Pináculo is clearly visible from the trig point. Continue down alongside a fence until you reach a style on the right but do not cross the style. Turn left here walking beside a water channel for a few metres before

The descent to Pináculo

Pináculo

crossing the channel and continuing down through the heathers until you finally reach Levada da Serra and a sign post on the levada path for Casa de Abrigo do Carmugo, another Forestry Post further west. The vegetation on the descent is quite barren, typical of the Paúl da Serra plateau, except that in June it has changed from its winter brown carpet to that of fresh green bracken, and an occasional rabbit, not too shy to put in an appearance for our benefit, was just an added bonus. Once on the path turn right to follow the levada downstream. The path has been formed on a ledge between the rock face and the mountain slopes of the São Vicente valley and as you progress ahead, views of Sugar Loaf and the high mountain peaks come into view through clearings in the vegetation, as do views of Vila de São Vicente and the coastline to the north. The route passes a number of semi circular rock walls, where waterfalls splash down into the levada and are caught by the sunlight, providing wonderful glistening sprays against the shiny rock face. The largest of these

'crashing over the levada'

resembles a small amphitheatre and here the largest waterfall crashes down over the levada. Eventually you reach the base of Pináculo; a lovely quiet place to stop for a picnic. For information only, at the base of Pináculo you will notice another path leading east, taking this would eventually lead you back to Encumeada. But let's leave that route for a future walk.

From Sugar Loaf you now retrace your steps back along the path until you pass the junction at the point where you joined the path. Now continue along the levada in the opposite direction crossing a bridged stream and another rock face. The path eventually begins a slight incline leaving the levada behind and crosses a number of smaller streams before the landscape begins to change from the lush vegetation to a dryer landscape now dominated by the Heather and Bilberry trees. A little further along you should now look out for a path on the left which zigzags up hill on a series of twisting steps and stones eventually leading you to a style. Once over the style carry on up hill through low vegetation following the fence and tree line, a total of 80 metres in all, until you finally return to the gate and official entrance of the Bica da Cana Forestry Post back on the ER110.

Alternative route:
For those not wanting to tackle the initial ascent to the Miradouro and the steeper descent down to the levada path, the walk to Sugar Loaf can be undertaken by walking the same route in both directions and thus minimising the ascent and descent. For this option follow the grassy path to the left of the main gates of the Forestry Post and continue down by the side of the fence and plantation until you reach the style. Turn left here, the path then drops down the stony staircase to a junction with another path. At this point turn right eventually picking up the levada and continue on to Pináculo. Return from here by the same route.

Two Walks in Encumeada

Walk 14   The Lily of the Valley Trail to Folhadal
Walk 15   Levada do Norte/Levada das Rabaças

Walking times:
Walk 1 - 1hr 50 mins return - Walk 2 - 2 hrs return
Grade:
Both are easy grade walks along wide level paths which follow the levadas. Walk 14 negotiates a 600 metre tunnel which is quite narrow with low head room along the first stretch but which soon widens out making for comfortable walking later. A torch is needed for this tunnel and there is a possibility of some dripping water in places, however this is minimal. All precipitous places are protected with fencing.
Directions and Starting Point:-
From the Rapido at Ribeira Brava follow the ER104 (São Vicente) taking the ER228 Serra de Água to Encumeada Pass (11 kms). At Encumeada go left for a few metres on to the ER110 parking at the Encumeada Gift Shop.

Both walks start opposite the snack-bar on the ER 228 just below the Encumeada gift shop and viewpoint from where, on a clear day, you can see both the north and south coast at São Vicente and Ribeira Brava. Taking a flight of steps up to Levada do Norte (signed 'Folhadal') now

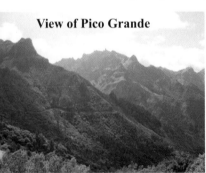

View of Pico Grande

follow the channel upstream along a wide path through a very pretty well planted area stocked with Lily of the Nile (Agapanthus) and Hydrangea. Within minutes you pass the levada keepers house on the right after which you take in magnificent views down the Ribeira Brava valley and east to Pico Grande. This mountain is easily recognised by the appearance of a rocky castle formation on the summit. The path then loops along the contours of the southern slopes of Encumeada and is flanked by natural vegetation; a particular beauty is the Pride of Madeira (Echium

Pride of Madeira

candicans) which is in bloom throughout the summer. This is the violet candle shaped flower which is endemic to Madeira. There are also many species of trees and other shrubs along the route including Laurel, Conifers, Oak, Cedar and Beech as well as Tree Heaths, Globe Flower and Melliferous Spurge. The latter two being endemic to Madeira and the Canaries. After approximately fifteen minutes you reach a tunnel entrance where Levada das Rabaças, which feeds Levada do Norte, now branches off.

Walk 14   The Lily of the Valley Trail to Folhadal

Continuing on Levada do Norte we now enter the 600 metre tunnel which takes us under Encumeada pass to the north of the island. The tunnel entrance is quite narrow and along the first stretch the rock is curved and requires a little stooping to avoid collision. However, a little further along the path widens and the height improves, making for much easier walking. A torch is definitely needed. This tunnel crosses from south to north under the ER 110 road which leads up to Paúl da Serra. Once through you exit on to a

wide path and at this point find yourself deep in the Madeira Laurisilva with its prehistoric vegetation and damp humid conditions. The contrasts between the north and south of the island are quite amazing; not only in the vegetation but also in the climate change, which can vary as much as 10 degrees in the short distance from one end of the tunnel to the other. Now having left the sunny south with its open vistas you find yourself in a green jungle high above the São Vicente valley. Nevertheless, the levada path is still

Lily-of-the-Valley

planted with Agapanthus and Hydrangea but now also many wild flowers and endemic species can be found. Depending on the time of the year you will be rewarded with sightings of wild orchids; mountain stocks, wild geraniums; St. John's Wort, giant thistles and dandelion trees just to mention a few. But most rewarding on this route is the existence of many Lily of the Valley trees (the local name is Folhados) from which this area takes its name. This tree is endemic to Madeira and when in flower between late August and early October, is really beautiful with its many white scented flowers. Apparently the locals use different parts of this tree for cattle fodder when grass is scarce and for making walking sticks from the straight new branches. From here

view down to north coast

you continue along the irrigation channel path which winds around the valley head and occasionally, when the vegetation open up, allows wonderful views down to the north coast and São Vicente. From this point you can make out the well known landmark of Nossa Senhora de Fátima, the distinctive church tower which sits on a ridge against a backdrop of green mountains and overlooks São Vicente.

After twenty minutes the path goes through another very short tunnel (no need for a torch here) and after another 200 mtrs reaches the entrance to a much longer tunnel. This is where the walk ends and from here you retrace your steps back to Encumeada. But first take a rest and refreshments here, the vegetation at this point is

short tunnel

so tropical and varied and to the left a large waterfall tumbles down the rock face before falling under the levada and down into the valley below. Continuing along this route through the tunnel would take you through another five tunnels to the Levada Keepers house at Folhadal from where you could either descend to Ginhas in the São Vicente valley or ascend up to Paúl da Serra at Bica da Cana and onto Pináculo which featured in Walk 13.

Walk 15   Levada do Norte/Levada das Rabaças

Back at the division of the levadas, fifteen minutes after leaving Encumeada and where Levada do Norte continues through the tunnel, continue now following Levada das Rabaças. This path, lies at 1000 mtrs above sea level looking down on Serra de Água and you can see the ER228 as it snakes down the valley passing the Residential Encumeada Hotel and on to the coast. The views from here are so wonderful as the vegetation is much less dense, so the peaks to the west and east and the coast to the south are always in view. The route continues for a further 40 minutes eventually going through a gate and passing a gorge to the right where a number

Lily of the Nile

of waterfalls cascade down from the Encumeada road above. A little further along you reach a tunnel entrance where you turn round and return to the starting point. These are both easy grade walks in stunning locations and are suitable for all ages and abilities. Continuing along the levada from here is pointless unless you are looking for a real challenge. The first tunnel is around 200 mtrs long followed soon after by the entrance to another tunnel of 2 kms in length, the longest accessible levada tunnel on the island. This is referred to in Walk 11 which approaches from the opposite direction from Cristo Rei via Cascalha. So again I am going to leave this for another day. However, continuing from here is definitely not for the faint-hearted as the route negotiates a number of narrow and quite dangerous unprotected sections. In addition it also requires a climb of 350 mtrs to bring you to Levada da Bica da Cana before ending on the ER 209 just below the Cristo Rei Statue on the edge of Paúl da Serra. Altogether it's a strenuous five hour walk but I hope to attempt this at some point in the future, although from choice, I would do it in reverse to avoid the ascent. So age and stamina permitting, "watch this space".

Shirley Whitehead's Madeira Walks

Walk 16   Boca da Corrida
to Pico Grande

Walking Time:
Allow 2½ hours- (8 kms return)

Grade:
A relatively strenuous walk along a mountain track with an initial ascent of just under 60 mtrs followed by a number of shorter ascents and descents along the route. Good paths with no precipitous places, but exposed mountain area which should only be undertaken in clear weather.

Directions and Starting Point:-
From Funchal follow the R101 in a westerly direction exiting at the sign for Estreito de Cãmara de Lobos. Now follow the ER229 as it climbs up to the centre of Estreito then take a right turn signed Jardim da Serra. From here the road continues to climb, eventually reaching the Casa Florestal at Boca da Corrida. A total of 10.2 kms from the Rapido. Parking is available beside the Forestry House.

The walk starts from the car park and picnic area of the Casa Florestal at Boca da Corrida on a mountain ridge above Estreito da Cãmara de Lobos. The Forestry House stands at 1,235 mtrs above sea level and is surrounded by sweet chestnut and conifer woodland and within its confines is a lovely shrine dedicated to São Cristovão. This is a really pretty area and a little haven before you venture out into the mountains. However, before starting the walk it is worthwhile taking a short detour on a path to the right of the car park which leads to a

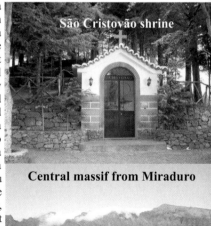

São Cristovão shrine

Central massif from Miraduro

Miradouro. From here the views are truly magnificent and set the scene for what you are about to encounter along this walk. The north eastern vista takes in all the main peaks of the central massif as well as the great depression of Curral das Freiras (Nun's Valley) where you can clearly see the parish scattered along the valley bottom. To the south lies São Martinho and the coast of Funchal and to the north west Pico Grande dominates the skyline. This is a Miradouro not to be missed.

Back at the car park, now follow the broad track to the left between the house and chapel and after approximately 15 mtrs take a narrow path uphill which soon climbs a series of stone steps. After a steady climb of 10 minutes, Pico Grande (at 1,657 mtrs) now towers ahead and is unmistakable due to the rocky castle-like formation on the summit. A little later the path levels out as it follows a wide ridge crossing a number of times from east to west thus providing magnificent view of both Curral das Freiras and the Encumeada Pass; from here on clear days you can see the wind turbines on the Paúl da Serra plateau.

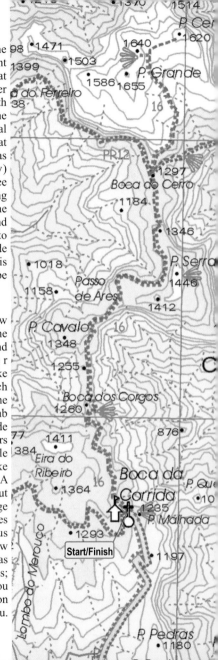

The track also passes a number of steep ravines, many bearing a small copse of Sweet Chestnut, giving a refreshing relief to what would otherwise be a barren landscape. At a later point the path passes below a high rock wall where Tree Heaths and Pride of Madeira (Echium candicans) cling to the sloping hillside. This latter plant is the mountain variety of the two Echiums endemic to Madeira and is usually a deeper colour with longer inflorescences than its sister plant (Echium nervosum) which appears nearer the coast. After a total of 45 minutes the stony track now makes a descent down to a natural

Looking down on Curral das Freiras

land bridge at Passo de Ares which is a narrow strip dividing the Brava and Socorridos river valleys. From here the path again traverses the eastern flank of the ridge passing a number of rocky outcrops below Pico do Serradinho before circling back to the western flank now providing good views down to Serra de Água and Vinháticos. From here you can pick out the ER228 as it climbs past the Residential Encumeada Hotel. Eventually after a total walking time of 1¼ hours you find yourself at Boca do Cerro just below

Pico Grande

the summit of Pico Grande and the continuing pathway can be clearly seen cut into the rock face below the mountain before making its descent to Encumeada. This route follows an old mule track, which in the past brought travellers from the north of the island to Câmara de Lobos. Lucky for us that we now only walk for pleasure! At this point we now find ourselves beside a sign directing us right, which climbs up to Chão de Relva from where one can then continue climbing to the summit of Pico Grande; a demanding and difficult climb taking another hour or so, or alternatively it is possible to descend into Curral das Freiras, by what appears to be another rather torturous route.

Obviously, there are many mountain trails on Madeira, but unfortunately many are more suited to the experienced walker However, due to the easy access to this walk and the relatively short ascents and descents, this route, whilst still challenging, is suitable for the less experienced and so enables us to enjoy the spectacular mountains views from this high altitude. Saying that however, Boca do Cerro was my chosen destination and on reaching that point I was satisfied that I had achieved my target and was happy to retrace my steps and enjoy the different perspectives of the return journey.

Spring is definitely the best time to undertake this walk. Not only to take advantage of the abundance of wild flora, at its best between March and June, but also to avoid the heat of summer when the landscape becomes arid and the route offers little protection against the summer sun. So if you want to get close to nature and enjoy a wonderful and challenging walk in this remote area then make sure you choose a clear day, take plenty of drinks and a picnic and I guarantee that you will have a wonderful walk and be rewarded with spectacular views from every vantage point.

After completing the walk and returning to the comfort of your transport, there is a final treat in store for those interested in Portuguese architecture. On the descent from the Forestry House, keep a look out for Quinta do Jardim da Serra, a three-stored pink Mansion House which was formerly the country estate of the rich and influential Englishman Henry Veitch. Veitch was Consul General on the island from 1809 – 1836 and as well as his political interests, he was also a wine merchant and architect of the Madeira

Quinta
Jardim da Serra

Wine Museum and was said to be instrumental in the building of the English Church and Graveyard in Funchal. The Quinta was originally surrounded by exotic cultivated gardens against a backdrop of forests and mountains but the original magnificent setting now has to be imagined due to the unsympathetic design of an adjacent modern block. Nevertheless, the beautiful Quinta still stands within an area of original garden and is well worth a visit by those interested in Madeira's history and architecture.

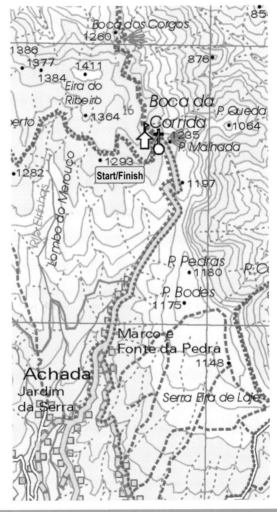

Walk 17   Ponta de São Lourenço Peninsula
– Baia d'Abra to Casa do Sardinha

Walking time:
2hrs 30 mins return
Grade:
A strenuous walk, good footwear is essential. A number of ascents and descents sometimes over rocky slopes. Care needed on the short detours to northern viewpoints which are unprotected. Otherwise other precipitous places are fenced.
Directions and Starting Point:-
Follow the R101 via the airport to Caniçal and continue on the new section of the highway which now by-passes Machico. Approximately 12 kms after the airport you reach a roundabout at the Industrial Zone and Port of Caniçal. From here follow the signs for Prainha and Ponta de São Lourenço. The walk starts from the road end car park at Baia d'Abra.

Madeira has so much to offer those who enjoy the beautiful and diverse scenery of the island and this walk provides a wonderful alternative to the lush forest and levada walks. The scenery is breathtaking and the landscape wild and rocky with rugged and exposed cliffs and coves carved out by the sea. The rock formations are truly amazing, with basalt veins or dykes running down through the multicoloured layers of volcanic rock. Also, unlike the rest of the island, this long narrow peninsula is much drier due to its low hills and so provides a habitat for a number of Madeira's rare and endemic plants. The best time to visit is in spring when the landscape is greener and the flora is at its best. In mid summer the grassland becomes arid and brown and there is no shelter from the blazing sun along the whole of the route, Nevertheless whatever time of year you choose, try to avoid a day when there is a haze or heavy cloud over the sea, then the whole landscape will be enhanced by a background of sparkling blue sea and blue sky.

This is a very popular walk, however it is quite strenuous and good footwear is essential. The path zigzags across the peninsula from south to north taking in views of the magnificent coast line along its route. In places you find yourself clambering over rocky ridges where the path often becomes vague, although white topped way markings and cairns clearly direct the route. In other places the path is along rocky mule tracks, but it is not a dangerous walk providing you keep to the paths and take care on the short detours which lead to the spectacular views of the northern bays.

Leaving the car park, walk between two large boulders and descend on a gravel path to the right into a small valley. From here you can take in the view of Baia d'Abra and looking across the peninsula you will see a circular rock arch over the water, above which is a small mountain. This lies beyond Casa do

Baia d'Abra

Rock tower

Sardinha, our destination. Continue up the hill and around the next bend and from here take a short left detour to your first viewpoint on the north coast. In this rocky bay, a 30m high rock tower rises up out of the water; it is quite

staggering. Back at the fork, the path begins a short steep ascent and climbs over a rocky slope. When I visited in spring the whole hillside was a picture, with a mass of Chrysanthemums, lilac Madeira Sea Stock (Matthiola maderensis)

South coast

and Madeira Marigolds (Calendula maderensis) the latter two being endemic to Madeira. Around the next corner you come to the second viewpoint, another spectacular bay with amazing rock formations. From here the path follows a wide arc around the

Natural land bridge

southern slopes and at a point approximately level with the floating fish farm, descends down to a natural land bridge which is the narrowest point on the peninsula, with 100m drops on either side down to the sea. However, it is very well protected with wire safety fencing so there is no real danger. From here you have excellent views of the whole land strip including the lighthouse on Ilhéu do Farol, a separate islet at the far end of the peninsula. Also in view are the

Ilhas das Desertas further out to sea, and on a clear day, good views of Porto Santo to the north east. In April the route was adorned with an array of other wonderful plants including the endemic Everlasting (Helichrysum devium) This is a small shrub with white and brown cups set into soft grey green velvety leaves, and not only is it endemic to Madeira, but also to Ponta de São Lourenço. Other species in abundance were the Purple Viper's Bugloss ((Echium plantagineum) related to the endemic Pride of Madeira, which is also present in its rarer white form, and the Ice Plant (Mesembryanthemum nodiflorum) a small white icy flower head with green and red basal leaves which is related to the garden variety of Mesembryanthemum. In former times, and during the Second World War, this plant was cultivated on the island for its soda content which was used in the production of soap.

From the land bridge it is then a short distance before Casa do Sardinha comes into view. This is a small single storey building with a terracotta tiled roof and was once a private dwelling reached by boat at the nearby jetty. The house, now a centre for the Reserva Natural da Ponta de São Lourenço guards, is surrounded by a small garden with giant

Casa do Sardinha

Date Palms, Cycads and Tamarisk trees and stands out like an oasis in the dry grassy landscape and rocky terrain.

This is definitely one of my favourite walks on the island; it is an unforgettable experience and a must for anyone who enjoys walking and the natural environment. Other than the occasional aircraft making its final ascent, which can be quite spectacular, the area is otherwise quiet and peaceful with only the sounds of birds to break the silence. Obviously there were many sea birds around and I was also lucky to get a glimpse of two other species of birds which inhabit this coastal zone, including a number of Canaries (Serinus canaria); these birds are the primitive form of the yellow caged variety, but the wild male bird has only a bright yellow chest whilst the female is more grey-brown. In addition I spotted a number of Berthelot's Pipit (Anthus berthelotii) which are endemic to Macaronesia occurring only in Madeira, the Canaries and the Selvagen Islands.

The return journey is by the same route, although from Case do Sardinha there are two further extensions to the walk. One is up a steep gritty path from the house to the summit of the nearby hill, with wonderful views of Ilhéu do Farol, Ilhas das Desertas and Porto Santo. (Allow another 1¼hrs return) The other leads down towards the rocky coast before heading back uphill to rejoin your original path for the return journey. I have to admit that at this point I did not have the energy to continue and was quite content to have reached my destination at Casa do Sardinha where I rested for a while before starting the journey back.

There are no refreshments to be found on this route, so be sure to take along plenty of drinks. However, once back at the car park you will find a mobile kiosk selling cold drinks and ice creams and believe me, at the end of this walk, a cold drink both for myself and for my dog Lucy, was very welcome indeed.

Note:
The peninsula is a protected area within the Parque Natural da Madeira, which ensures that all endemic plants are protected by law. Shortly after the beginning of the walk you will pass a sign which clearly indicates that the area is a zone for the recuperation of flora and in certain places footpaths have been diverted away from the eroded areas where plants are being re-established. It is extremely important to keep to these diversions.

Two walks in Ribeira de São Roque Valley – Faial

Walk 18 - Levada do Castelejo
Walk 19 - Levada de Baixo

Walking times:
Walk 18 - 2hrs 30 mins return. Walk 19 - 2 hrs circular walk
Grade:
Both easy walking along the levada shoulder. Some slightly precipitous sections along Levada do Castelejo and an ascent of 100 mtrs from Levada do Baixo to Lombo Grande
Directions and Starting Point:
Taking the Rapido R101 from the airport follow the signs for Porto da Cruz and Santana. Once through Machico join the new northern highway ER101 for approx. 10 kms. 2.3 kms past Porto da Cruz take the ER217, a left turn signed São Roque de Faial
Walk 18 - At this junction make a U-turn back onto the ER101 and take the first right immediately before the tunnel, signed Porto do Cruz. (turning left immediately after the tunnel is not permitted). This road climbs up to Cruz village; take a right turn signed Levada do Castelejo. The levada is approx 1 km along this road keeping to the right. Parking is available close by.
Walk 19 - Continue up the ER217. The road twists and climbs for 2 kms arriving at the Sanroque bar, restaurant and tourist hotel. Parking is available at this point.

The Ribeira de São Roque valley rises from the foot of Penha de Águia (Eagle Rock) and extends to the north eastern slopes of the central massive below Pico da Suna close to Ribeira Frio. To the west lie the slopes of Pico dos Torros and Pico do Ruivo. In addition, Eagle Rock provides a magnificent backdrop to both walks; this landmark towering above the coast between Porto da Cruz and Faial. The vegetation in this mountainous landscape is natural and lush as the routes transcends through the São Roque valley into the Laurisilva. Walk 18 starts above the hamlet of Cruz and walk 19 from São Roque do Faial village; both levadas lying at approx 350 mtrs above sea level.

Walk 18 - Levada do Castelejo

The hamlet of Cruz lies on a mountain ridge above Porto da Cruz and the Levada do Castelejo can be picked up at a point just above the village. From here follow the channel upstream through agricultural terraces and vineyards soon going round a sharp bend as you wind your way into the São Roque valley. At this point you look across at the picturesque village of São Roque do Faial set against a backdrop of mountains; to the north is Eagle Rock and the sea. Soon you leave the agricultural slopes behind and wind your way along the rocky valley side into the lush vegetation of the Laurisilva when magnificent views of the mountains come clearly into view. The valley here is deep and across on the other side the Levada de Baixo is clearly visible, as is the high waterfall of Água D'Alto as it crashes over the valley side into the São Roque river. Large sections of the levada are carved into the rock where water drops

Penha de Águia

Levada do Castelejo

from the rock face providing an ideal habitat for the rich and varied ferns and mosses that can be found here. As you get further into the valley, the vegetation is dominated by Laurel, Willow, Tree Heath and Mimosa; the latter was in flower at the time of my visit, filling the air with its wonderful scent. Along the route, the paths are flanked with Bramble, Gorse, Giant Reed and Taro Root and wild flowers were in abundance, providing a lovely contrast. The path is narrow in places and whilst reasonably good, there are a number of precipitous places along the route and great care should be taken negotiating these sections. However, much of the levada and path are currently undergoing restoration and protective fencing is being erected on the dangerous sections. The route contours a number of lush side valleys before narrowing as you approach the river bed and the source of the levada. This is a beautiful location to stop for a picnic where the river tumbles over huge boulders and forms pools in the rocky bed. From here you retrace your steps, however it is possible to wander a little further up the river on a narrow left hand path which brings you to a number of rushing waterfalls where you can further enjoy the tranquility and beauty of this location before returning.

Walk 19 - Levada de Baixo

This walk starts and ends at the Sanroque Hotel and Restaurant in the small agricultural village of São Roque de Faial. Arlindo, the proprietor and Mayor of the village, speaks good English and has good local knowledge of the area. The path to Levada de Baixo/Água D'Alto starts a few metres above the Sanroque Hotel, signed left off the road. This is a narrow levada set into the western terraces of the deep valley. Levada de Baixo flows from Agua D'Alto, a smaller valley to the right of Ribeira do São Roque valley. Following the path upstream, the levada contours the valley side and terraces, passing many traditional A shaped farm buildings and orchards, with a vast array of fruit and vegetable plantations. Mango, Custard Apple, Avocado and Loquat present themselves along the route, as do Bananas, Sugar Cane, small vineyards and vegetable crops. The plantations are neat and well

Calla Lily

tended with Agapanthus and Hydrangea introduced along the path and a little further along the natural vegetation takes over. My husband and I walked this route in early March when the distant mountains were covered in snow and were looking particularly beautiful, but in spite of the cold weather, this valley lies in a sheltered position from the wind, so on the day of our visit it felt as balmy and warm as an English summer's day, with many butterflies and lizards to take our interest. In both locations there was a predominance of white Eupatorium and many species of the

pea family (Fabaceae). The spring flowering Three-Cornered Leek (Allium triquetrum) was growing in abundance displaying its lovely white flower heads and Red Flowering Sorrel (Oxalis purpurea), Violets, Scarlet Pimpernel and the large white Calla Lilies (Calla aethiopica) were just a few of the many flowers to be seen. We also found the bright green Navelwort growing from the rocky crevices. This latter plant has lush green leaves which resemble the human navel, hence its name (Umbilicus rupestris).

Agua d'Alto

Levada de Baixo is approximately 2 kms long and as the path nears the valley head Água D'Alta comes clearly into view as it tumbles down small waterfalls before crashing down into the São Roque river. On reaching the source of the levada, the path crosses the river and from here gradually ascends to the left up a series of broad steps and slopes to the hamlet of Lombo Grande, standing at 450 metres on a high plateau between the two valleys. At this point you now find yourself on the edge of the natural forest and I was delighted to see the Tree Heath in flower. On arriving in Lombo Grande the vistas open up to the north east coast with magnificent views of Penha de Águia. From here you pick up a tarred road for approx 1.8kms which

Pathway to Lombo Grande

twists and turns through the forest, climbing another 40 mtrs until it eventually meets the ER217. At the junction turn right and descend down the hill back to your starting point at São Roque, a distance of just under 2 kms. At this higher level the mountain landscape to the west is clearly visible as are the north east coastal villages of Faial and Porto da Cruz

Porto da Cruz

On your return from either of these walks, why not also combine the day out with a visit to Porto da Cruz. This small, yet lively fishing village, is set in a beautiful location with stunning views of the north coast from its harbour. Also of interest is the newly erected statue, a tribute to the Lavadeiros (Levada Workers). The statue stands in the centre of the roundabout as you enter the village and has been erected in recognition of the thousands of men, who over a period of 500 years, laboured to create the levada network; a unique monument and so important to Madeira's cultural heritage.

Walking Time:
Allow 3 ½ hours (one way)

Grade:
A reasonably long and mildly strenuous walk along a very well trodden route at first on a wide level path which then becomes narrower and stony further along. Precipitous places are protected by fencing. There is a descent of approximately 190 mtrs along the final 2 km stretch. Ribeiro Frio stands at 860 mtrs while Portela lies at 670 mtrs.

Directions and Starting Point:-
From the Rapido R101 east of Funchal, take either the ER103 via Monte continuing through Poiso to the village of Ribeiro Frio. Alternatively, take the new road to Camacha turning left before the town and picking up the ER203 to Poiso, then connecting with the ER103 to Ribeiro Frio. Roadside parking is available beside the bars and restaurants in the village centre.

Ribeiro Frio is a small hamlet and one of the most popular tourist destinations on the island due to its stunning location on the northern slopes of the highest peaks, whilst nestling deep within the largest area of Madeira's Laurisilva. The centre boasts many attractions including a trout farm and a nature conservation area, as well as gift shops, restaurants and bars where the visitor can buy freshly smoked trout or sample a glass of Poncha, the famous honey and aguardente tonic, guaranteed to warm walkers throughout the winter months. The centre is also the starting point for a shorter spectacular trail to Balcões where, when the mists permit, you can take in magnificent views Pica Arieiro (1816m), Pico do Gato (1782m), Pico das Torres (1852m) and Pico Ruivo (1862m).

The walk starts from the village centre just below Victor's Bar where a new sign directs us down a path over the Ribeiro Frio (Cold River). This route crosses one of the largest and most well preserved areas of the island's indigenous forests, first following a broad path which soon picks up the Levada do Furada. The route is beautiful and full of interest as we follow the levada downstream, sometimes walking through the dark and humid primitive forest with its rich subtropical vegetation, and at other times in lighter

Levada do Furado

sunnier woodland. The path meanders under the tree canopy between rock cuttings and rocky slopes which often overhang and where rivulets drip into the levada providing a habitat for a vast array of large ferns, mosses and lichens. The route is green, damp and humid, trout dart around in the levada; and providing there are not too many walkers around, you will see many birds, butterflies and insects as you walk along. After a short distance huge boulders appear, followed by a long protected section before we eventually reach Cabeço Pessequeiro to get our first view of a vast area of the forest canopy together with views of Faial and Penha de Águia (Eagle Rock) on the north coast. A little further along we reach Ribeira do Beserro where a bridge

crosses the gorge; many walkers stop here for a picnic and the birds have become so tame that they will come quite close to share your crumbs. At this point two narrow channels feed into the levada from the right, providing another circular walk back to Ribeiro Frio. This walk leads you deep into the forest on a 330 mtr ascent to eventually arrive higher up the ER103. However, we ignore this and continue over the bridge and progress a little further along the path to where a section of the levada shoulder has become damaged. This necessitates a short detour down a stony slope which crosses the riverbed before rejoining the levada path. Here you will find a lovely little pond

Cabeço Pessequeiro

Levada Tunnel

near to which I stumbled across two endemic species of the forest; the very rare Yellow Foxglove (Isoplexis sceptrum) and the Lily

Yellow Foxglove

of the Valley Tree (Clethra arborea). The former is found only in the Laurisilva, growing in ravines and rocky slopes and unlike its close family member the Digitalis Purpurea, (the common purple European foxglove), this species grows to the size of a small tree. The Lily of the Valley Tree flowers from late August to October and can be identified at this time by its beautiful and numerous fragrant white flowers.

From here on, the walk takes on a different perspective as the path winds its way through a rocky gorge and a large number of short tunnels and archways cut into the rock where rustic steps and handrails have been erected. Here the levada is curving around Cabeço Furada before it eventually leads us to the Lamaceiros

Water House. This 100 year old building is set in a small mysterious clearing where a number of huge old oak trees stand proudly, obviously introduced at around the same period. A little further along, we meet a crossroads signed Santo da Serra, Camacha and Portela. We leave the levada here and take a left turn down the stepped path picking up the narrow Levada da Portela flowing on the left of the track and soon we reach the Lamaceiros Forestry Post. This is set in an enchanting, more formal forest area with lovely gardens, where you will find picnic tables set amidst mighty Cedars and tropical Tree Ferns. The road from the Forestry

Lamaceiros Water House

Lamaceiros

The junction

Post now leads us down to a junction. Turning left we follow the narrow levada on a long descent, first passing an estate on the right, the first signs of habitation since we left Ribeira Frio, and then continuing through an area of mature pines and mimosa trees. Looking north at this point we can take in magnificent views of the coastline at Porto do Cruz and get a much clearer view of Eagle Rock which now dominates the vista. Continuing on from here we eventually reach the ER102 at Portela where there is a taxi rank and bus stop beside the Miradouro da Portela Bar and Restaurant.

APPENDICES

APPENDIX A

Useful Information

Contacts

The following information is believed to be correct at the time of printing. However, if you have difficulty contacting any of the agencies referred to, I suggest you contact the tourist office or ask for assistance from your hotel reception staff.

Note:
The dial code for Madeira when calling from overseas is 00-351

SPEA-Madeira – The Portuguese Society for the Protection of Birds
Travessa das Torres
Old Town, 9060-314 Funchal
Telephone: 291 241 210
E-mail: Madeira@spea.pt
www.spea.pt

Parque Natural da Madeira
Telephone:: 291 214 360
E-mail: pnm@gov-madeira.pt

For information on the Desertas Islands
E-mail: rosapires.sra@gov-madeira.pt

The Madeira Times
Telephone: 291 85 93 061
www.themadeiratimes.com

Main Tourist Office Funchal
Avenida Arriago No 18
Telephone: 291 211 902
E-mail: info@madeira.tourism.org
www.madeiratourism.org

- Emergencies   112

- Police   291 700 112

- Red Cross   291 741 115

Taxis

Estrela da Calheta	**96 6038 547**
	91 9695 861
Calheta	**291 822129**
Camacha	**291 822125**
Cãmara de Lobos	**291 945229**
	291 942144
	291 942407
Campanario	**291 953601**
Caniçal	**291 961989**
Caniço	**291 934640**
	291 934606
Canhas	**91 9514 041**
Faial	**291 572416**
Funchal - Central	**291 222500**
- Avenida do Mar	**291 224588**
- Mercada	**291 226400**
- Martinho	**291 765620**
- Nazaré	**291 762780**
Guala	**291 526643**
Machico	**291 962480**
	291 962189
	291 962220
Monte	**291 782158**
Ponto do Sol	**291 972110**
Porto da Cruz	**291 562411**
Paúl do Mar	**96 3075 612**
Porto Moniz	**291 852243**
Ponto do Pargo	**96 5013 090**
- Amparo	**96 7425 752**
- Cabo	**291 882165**
Ribeira Brava	**291 951800**
Ribeiro Frio	**291 782158**
Santa Cruz	**291 524888**
Santana	**291 572540**
Santo da Serra	**291 522100**
São Vicente	**291 842238**

APPENDIX B

Recommended Reading

Reference Books

For those interested in the flora and fauna of the island I recommend the following publications which I have found invaluable in identifying species and understanding and familiarizing myself with Madeira's natural history.

- Flora Endémica da Madeira – Roberto Jardim/David Fransisco
  Pub.2000 – ISBN 972-8622-00-7
- Madeira Plants and Flowers – L.O. Franquinho/A. Da Costa
  Pub.1999 – ISBN 972-9177-21-X
- Madeira's Natural History in a Nutshell – Peter Sziemer
  Pub.2000 – ISBN 972-9177-31-7
- Madeira – A Botanical Melting Pot – Dr Susanne Lipps
  Pub.2006 – ISBN 3-938282-09-6

Publications

SPEA-Madeira – Discover the Birds of Laurissilva IBA (and surrounding areas)
Discover the Birds of Ponta do Pargo IBA

Maps

Madeira Tour & Trail Super-Durable Map
(ISBN 1-904946-26-7) £7.99
pub.2006 Discovery Walking Guides Ltd.
Latest 4th Edition, recognized by the 'Yellow Flash'on its cover, is the best map of Madeira you can buy. Large 1:40,000 scale, combined with the latest ground survey information, modern design techniques and Super-Durable material mean that you get both the latest and toughest map available. Nothing else on the market even comes close for value, accuracy, clarity and usability.

Madeira Bus & Touring Map
(ISBN 1-904946-09-7) £2.50
pub. 2005 Discovery Walking Guides Ltd.
Madeira buses are a popular way to see the island. Suitable for bus users and car drivers. A good way to plan your Madeiran adventures.

Guide Books

Walk! Madeira
(ISBN 1-904946-24-0) £12.99
 pub. 2006 Discovery Walking Guides Ltd.
David & Ros Brawn's latest book contains 36 fully detailed walking routes with full colour 1:25,000 scale Tour & Trail mapping and photos. Wire-O spiral binding allows the book to lay-flat when reading and be folded-back on itself in use. Walk! Madeira replaces their very popular '35 Madeira Walks' guide book.

Landscapes of Madeira
Sunflower Books
The latest edition of the 'little blue book' by John & Pat Underwood that introduced us all to Madeira so many years ago.
If you are not buying a DWG book then Landscapes is the next choice.

Join us for loads more walking
adventures using

Discovery Walking Guides

maps and guide books.
'Leaders in Walking Navigation at
Home & Abroad'

WALK! UK SERIES

160 full colour pages spiral bound £12.99 each

1-904946-10-0	Walk! The Yorkshire Dales (North & Central)
1-904946-11-9	Walk! The Peak District (South)
1-904946-13-5	Walk! The South Pennines
1-904946-14-3	Walk! The South Downs
1-904946-15-1	Walk! The Lake District North
1-904946-16-X	Walk! The Lake District South
1-904946-17-8	Walk! The Brecon Beacons
1-904946-20-8	Walk! Dorset
1-904946-12-7	Walk! Dartmoor
1-904946-18-6	Walk! Exmoor

SPANISH MAINLAND & ANDORRA

1-904946-23-2	Walk! the Alpujarras	£12.99
1-904946-25-9	Alpujarras Tour & Trail Map 2nd ed	£7.99
1-904946-04-6	Walk! Andorra	£11.99
1-904946-08-9	Walk! Axarquía	£11.99
1-899554-96-3	Sierra de Aracena	£11.99
1-899554-97-1	Sierra de Aracena Tour & Trail Map £2.99	

CANARY ISLANDS

1-899554-90-4	Walk! La Gomera (2nd Ed.) £11.99
1-899554-91-2	La Gomera T&T Super-Durable Map £7.99
1-899554-55-6	Drive! La Gomera Touring Map £2.50
1-899554-94-7	Walk! Lanzarote £11.99
1-899554-95-5	Lanzarote Tour & Trail Super-Durable Map £7.99

| 1-904946-06-2 | Walk! La Palma | £11.99 |
| 1-904946-07-0 | La Palma Tour & Trail Super-Durable Map | £7.99 |

1-904946-27-5	Walk! Tenerife	£12.99
1-904946-29-1	Tenerife Hiking Map	£3.50
1-904946-28-3	Tenerife Bus & Touring Map	£2.50

MADEIRA

1-904946-24-0	Walk! Madeira	£12.99
1-904946-26-7	Madeira T&T Super-Durable Map	£7.99
1-904946-09-7	Madeira Bus & Touring Map	£2.50
1-904946-31-3	Shirley Whitehead's Madeira Walks	£7.99

BALEARIC ISLANDS

1-904946-19-4	Walk! Mallorca (North & Mountains) 2nd Ed. Spiral Bound	£12.99
1-899554-93-9	Mallorca North & Mountains Tour & Trail Super-Durable Map	£7.99
1-899554-98-X	Walk! Mallorca (West)	£11.99

| 1-904946-02-X | Walk! Menorca | £11.99 |
| 1-904946-03-8 | Menorca Tour & Trail Super-Durable Map | £7.99 |

GPS NAVIGATION

| 1-904946-30-5 | Personal Navigator Files version 3.02CD | £9.99 |
| 1-904946-22-4 | GPS The Easy Way (2nd edition) | £4.99 |

All DWG titles are available from bookshops or 'post free' from

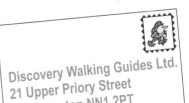

Discovery Walking Guides Ltd.
21 Upper Priory Street
Northampton NN1 2PT